About the Author

Throughout the course of his youth and adult life George has been focused on the interface between the psychology of Carl Jung and Christian spirituality. This has been expressed first in priestly ministry and spiritual direction, and now in psychotherapy, counselling, peace and nonviolence education and artwork. George is committed to promoting Jung's psychological insights as contemporary spiritual practice for the wellbeing of individuals and for the common good. He lives in Western Australia.

georgetrippe@gmail.com
website: TrippeArt.com

Who Said That?

The Spirited Practice of Active Imagination

George E. Trippe, PhD

First published 2022 by George E. Trippe, PhD

Produced by Independent Ink
independentink.com.au

Cover design by Independent Ink
Internal design by Independent Ink
Typeset in 12.5/17 pt Adobe Garamond Pro by Post Pre-press Group, Brisbane
Cover image: by the author

ISBN 978-0-6454243-4-8 (paperback)
ISBN 978-0-6454243-5-5 (epub)

Disclaimer:
Any information in the book is purely the opinion of the author based on personal experience and should not be taken as business or legal advice. All material is provided for educational purposes only. We recommend to always seek the advice of a qualified professional before making any decision regarding personal and business needs.

Contents

Introduction

Finding herself home in the isolation period of the 2020 Coronavirus event, my long time friend and former client, Leigh, decided to review some of her old journals. She came across the one from 1991 in which she had recorded her active imagination dialogues. This was during the times of our conversations. She used the dialogues to help her address the stresses she was experiencing both in her workplace and personal life. In a recent email Leigh writes: "So, this afternoon, I read through a journal from '91 of Active Imagination dialogues. Imagine! Perhaps you will recall (or not), I was working with you at that time and trying to find my way through a thorny situation at [her workplace]. I was taken aback by the depth of those internal conversations, the "wisdom" that came forth. Truly, a powerful tool for knowing oneself and uncovering hidden perspectives."

After twenty-nine years these active imagination dialogues still evoked a significant emotional response. Her response affirms the truth that, for many who will make the effort to engage this form of inner conversation, the experience of active imagination is deeply meaningful and has the potential to create change and long lasting influence.

My own experience with active imagination began in 1977. My first encounter was a dialogue with an old woman who was following me. The second was with a grizzly bear that I share in chapter four. I was quickly convinced of the importance and benefits of these experiences. Since then I have been grateful for the richness and insight these dialogues contribute to my well-being as part of my spiritual practice. Like Leigh, I am amazed at the wisdom that emerges from these experiences, both in the original encounter, and many years later in review. I am forever grateful to my analyst at that time, Weyler Greene, for suggesting that I try to talk with the woman and then with the bear. The conversations over years have included times of consolation, comfort, challenges, arguments, yelling matches, and the emergence of new ways of looking at my life. Through the dialogues I have developed an image of my soul as a village made up of an amazing, colourful and complex family of villagers, who have become deeply satisfying companions. These encounters continue to be healing and deeply rewarding. The Afterword to this study offers further testimony to this fact.

This work is a study of active imagination as developed by Carl Jung and others who have developed their work in the tradition of Jung. My intention in creating this work is two fold. First, I write to honour this transformative and spirited experience that opens us to healing and life-changing dialogue with the unconscious. Second, I offer this study to promote active imagination as a vibrant and healing psycho-spiritual practice. Active imagination is a way to engage ourselves more deeply so that we live more peacefully with our own complexities. These remarkable dialogues help us befriend ourselves.

There are five chapters in this work. It is divided into two parts. In part one, chapter one, *The Practice of Active Imagination*, I define active imagination and explain the practice. In the second chapter, *Relating to the Experience*, I consider practical matters in using active imagination, and focus on the benefits of the experience. Part two of this study focuses on dialogues that people have shared with me over a number of years. In Chapter three, *The People we Are*, we review dialogues that involve conversations with inner characters, people of the village. In Chapter four, *Look Who's Talking: Other Voices*, we consider dialogues with animals and parts of our bodies, and in Chapter five, *Encounters with Sacred Images*, our focus is on dialogues with sacred images and the Voice.

At the outset I thank those who have offered their dialogue experiences for this study. All dialogues are presented under pseudonyms except my own. My hope is that these shared experiences will encourage others to take up the practice of active imagination, and from their own dialogues to come to a deeper sense of wholeness and internal peace. My experience affirms that befriending ourselves through this practice enables us to relate more deeply and peacefully, not only with ourselves, but with others as well. Active imagination, therefore, is a vital practice for both individual and collective healing.

Part One

We begin our journey into the world of active imagination by defining the practice and considering variations of the process. We will also consider the benefits of active imagination and review how to relate to the experience. Chapter one begins with Louisa's experience.

The Practice of Active Imagination

You can only be what you can imagine yourself to be.
Morton T. Kelsey

Shortly after Louisa came to see me, she realised that her marriage was collapsing and she needed to separate from her husband. It was a difficult realisation, and she was ambivalent about the decision for much of the time. A dream came in the midst of her turmoil that introduced the image of a lovely garden with a fountain. As dream figures continued to emerge, Louisa decided to enter conversations with them in active imagination. She chose to do this in the safe environment of her dream garden and invited them there for afternoon tea. Over time the group grew and for several months she continued to meet with them all at least weekly to discuss her circumstances. The growing group represented Louisa's very different and conflicted points of view. The garden setting gave her a way to engage with her own complex thoughts as she moved through those difficult days.

As we engage all the dialogues in this study, I have used these guidelines in presenting the texts. In textual quotations I replicate the spelling and punctuation of the original text. I leave spaces between words where there is no punctuation in the original text, and where punctuation would be appropriate. If clarification of the text is needed, brackets [ ] are used to include any additions to the text. I have used the asterisk [*] to edit words that usually do not appear literally in texts for general public reading. I <u>underline</u> words underlined in the original text, and use **bold** type for those words that are underlined twice. Brackets enclosing full stops [...] are also used to indicate deleted text. Three full stops ... are used to indicate pauses in quotations.

Louisa describes the characters who joined her for the tea party dialogues as follows:

<u>Army Captain</u> (AC): Emerged from recognising a large part of my behaviour/coping strategies in the marriage. Plus all the women in my family are captains.

<u>Nathanial</u> (N): A wonderful caring beautiful sensual man from a dream. He guided and supported me before other figures emerged.

<u>Little Louisa</u> (LL): Free spirit wise child emerged after the elevator dream.

<u>Cab Driver</u> (CB): Ocker Australian chauvinist pig good natured mate type. came from a dream.

<u>Scared One</u> (SO): Pale frightened terrified head bandaged from ECT's age 19 – emotionally 16.

<u>Traditional Girl</u> (TG): Convent good girl-marriage is forever-don't rock the boat.

Michael (M): a priest – from dreams.

Benedict (B): Originally came from [name] in a dream – renamed Benedict, similar to Michael.

Philomena (Phil): The one who wants change Radical Outspoken Attractive Empowered.

Anger (A): personified the feeling.

This is the first of Louisa's dialogues. The characters are sitting around a rectangular table in the garden. Louisa begins the conversation.

The Tea Party

L.   Thank you all for being here in my garden. I've asked all of you to give me some perspective and clarity on my marriage. I'm also asking you to be co-operative with each other so we can all hear each other's view point.

Phil.   I don't mind starting – I want some change, something different to happen; the old way went on far too long. Louisa, my advice is to stay with what is, no matter how difficult, and truth will emerge for you. Lots of change has happened and is still going on Have courage – don't cave in on yourself – you seem to lose your courage and panic. Change is essential. You have to know what you want, and what you don't.

CB.   God you are talking about a decent bloke here – What are you on about! The guy provides for her loves the kids, works hard and she up there (Louisa) takes it all for granted and creates difficulties that aren't even there. She probably crucifies the guy. Poor bugger – save me from bitches like her.

SO. I wouldn't hurt him. I just want harmony and a good man to take care of me and my kids. It's important to look alright and for the kids to have a normal home What do you expect – the world? You can't expect everything in a marriage, and you are dumb and can't do lots of things. How would you look after yourself if it wasn't for [husband]. He saved you from the gutter in the first place. Make amends, look after him and forget about yourself. You have enough! financial security, a great house, and great kids. You would be mad to change that, and how would you take care of yourself Answer that.

N. Well she's finding a new way. The old one doesn't apply anymore.

AC. I think you both need to smarten up. You need to pull him …

L. Please be quiet I've invited you along in a minor capacity, not to tell me how to run my life.

CB. You want to run everything – even forcing him to go to a therapist. The poor bugger just wants some peace.

L. I'm not forcing him he needs to go for himself.

CB. Smartarse – normal people don't need therapists Why can't you work things out for yourself

Phil. Because She's stifled not heard by men like you rulers of the world – so long as she's the good little girl, passive dumb wife, level of a servant generally, except when he feels generous and pretends it's a one to one relationship. There's other men around, you know they are not all like this guy here (cab driver). Anyway you need to learn to stand on your own two feet, and you can't with your marriage like this.

N. I support that. Keep your temper under control Louisa. Find a way you'll see much clearer then.

L. Little Louisa do you want to say anything?

LL. Just don't stay there if it's not right for me. We've only just got together after 41 years. Don't abandon me again.

SO. Go along with him You have done it all this time What's so different except in your mind? He hasn't changed.

Phil. No and he won't unless you do. Meditate each day stay tuned.

L. Thank you all. I have Philomena, Little Louisa, and Nathaniel all telling me to keep centred, know myself, have courage and journey on. I have the Scared One, and the Cab Driver telling me I'm stupid and ridiculous and to toe the line, with the Army Captain being irrelevant. Here is my priest coming late. Please come and sit down next to Nathaniel. Would you please tell me your name

M. It's Michael and I'm glad to be here.

L. Would you please tell me how you see my marriage?

M. You are not your marriage There is more to you than that. In many ways it is a good marriage, because you are both good and caring people, but the good marriage is only on the outside. The union inside doesn't exist. As I see it you are both unfulfilled and unhappy. You need to want to love each other to look and see who is there now. You are neither the same, meeting from the old way. You will both want to have commitment to each other to ride through this change. If one doesn't have that commitment to see if love can grow, it is over. Your marriage is in a shaky position. You cannot afford to ignore the changes. This is a crucial time My advice is to listen to yourself your higher self, ask for guidance when you need and go down this road. You have the courage to discover what is already there.

L.   Thank you Thank you all.

The setting of the garden and afternoon tea gave Louisa a container in which to hold and engage her very diverse and complex opinions in the midst of her process. These dialogue conversations gave Louisa a way to acknowledge consciously her different points of view and to chart her course forward with greater confidence. Her decision out of this work was to proceed with separation and divorce. The conscious companionship of her diverse inner characters enabled Louisa to live through these experiences with a deeper sense of peace and a trust in her own future.

Defining Active Imagination

Active imagination is a practice by which ego consciousness employs our imaginations to enter into dialogue with images that emerge from the unconscious. While the individual can design different methods or steps in using the process, it is, in essence, a spontaneous and creative function. The images engaged are symbolic of interior points of view residing in the unconscious. Often these images emerge through dream characters or fantasies with "others." They can also arise in any significant encounter in life that carries a charge of energy. Active imagination can serve us in exploring both crises and opportunities. We will return to this a little later on.

Dr. Carl Jung began to use the practice of active imagination as early as 1913 out of his own need to engage the images of his unconscious. Originally known as the "transcendent function," active imagination became the common term for the experience from the 1930s. Barbara Hannah in her work, *Encounters with the Soul*, stresses that Jung did not invent this method, but developed it out of his own need to relate to the images that were emerging from the unconscious. She also cites several examples of the practice that come from earlier and ancient times. John Sanford in his work *Mystical Christianity* posits the possibility that active imagination with the risen Christ is the primary source for the author of the Christian Gospel of John. In his gospel account the author presents material that differs significantly from the other three Gospels. Likewise, it is possible to wonder if the dialogue between Abraham and God in the biblical text beginning at Genesis 18:23 is from an active imagination dialogue between the author and the divine image. These examples help us see that active imagination has been used from ancient times for personal insight, healing and for relating to the gods. It is primarily through Jung's work that we owe its place among the ways today in which we relate to the inner life.

Active imagination is a meditation experience using images and narrative stories. In the tradition of meditation it is a form of kataphatic meditation as distinct from the apophatic tradition of imageless meditation. Active imagination may also be seen as a form of fantasy. Whether defined as meditation or fantasy, the key characteristic is that individual consciousness is active, focused with deliberate and prolonged concentration on, and engagement with, the images that provoke and inspire a response from us. The focus on the original image remains constant; we do not move away from the original image into passive fantasy with a chain of images. Any subsequent images that emerge remain attached to the original image like spokes are attached to the hub of a wheel. The original image, the one that caught our attention, is the image on which we remain centred in order to explore the significance and meaning that has attracted us.

Robert Johnson, in *Inner Work*, stresses the dialogic nature of the experience. The essential character of the experience is a mutual exchange with the unconscious through images. The dialogues in part two present a variety of images in the encounters. The important element is that the images are such that the individual can enter into robust dialogue with whatever or whoever comes forward.

As we shall see in later examples, our dialogues often involve engaging images that present ideas and opinions that differ significantly from our conscious point of view. These contrary images are some aspect of what Jung has named the Shadow. In soul work using dreams and active imagination Shadow images often come to consciousness as a way of offering balance and wholeness to the limited perspectives of our present consciousness. The challenge of active imagination in this regard is to risk suspending our usual rational point of view, while remaining fully conscious, attentive and ready to respond. In a sense we relativise the ego's role as the gatekeeper or controller of our conscious stance, and allow the inner images to speak and disclose their differing points of view. In these encounters we have the ongoing opportunity to learn about the Shadow, those previously ignored, hidden or unknown parts of ourselves.

Variations

The most common starting place for an active imagination dialogue is a dream or fantasy. As mentioned earlier, we can also use the experience to explore our response to any image that carries energy, including a person, and significant event, and to engage a mood or feeling that has caught hold of us. As noted, it is important to stay with the original image in active imagination, to circle around it, as it were, and to contend with whatever comes forward.

The actual practice of active imagination can vary greatly, and can include a variety of media for expression. The most common expression is the written dialogue that usually takes the form of a script between characters. Louisa's dialogue above is an example of this form. Variations for the process include painting, drawing, dancing or clay modelling as ways to give form or shape to the original image. I have found the experience of dance accompanied by simple chant to be a deeply moving experience of active imagination that makes sense and has coherence, even if I cannot explain it rationally. I have also found the creation of an artwork in collage a way to dialogue with the unconscious through the choice and placement of materials without a preconceived plan for the image. It can be a deeply meditative time to watch the formation of the image and the juxtaposition of the colours and textures. The experience may also take the form of a poem or the composition of a piece of music. The variations are really endless and depend on the individual. It seems possible that one who works in wood in the shed, or bakes in the kitchen, may find in these experiences a form of dialogue with the creative energy of the soul. It is possible the hands and the body often know how to address a mood, solve a riddle, open a path forward, or give insight that has escaped the understanding of the conscious mind. The process of expressing ourselves through these creative media not only releases creative energy, but also may assist us with the assimilation of unconscious contents into consciousness as we reflect quietly on our experience. I remember counselling an artist who found dream recall difficult, so he brought his quick sketches and spontaneous doodles for future artworks to our reflections. These were a valuable resource into his psychic process. Once we open ourselves to the dialogue between the unconscious and our conscious minds, it is both challenging and inspirational to consider the many forms the dialogue will take.

Two Distinctions

In defining active imagination, two important distinctions need to be made. The first is the difference between active imagination and passive imagination experiences. In the realm of the imagination and psychic experience, distinctions between active and passive imagination will remain somewhat blurred, yet there are distinctions in speaking about dreams, passive fantasy, and active imagination to consider. The essential distinction is the stance of the conscious ego. In our dreams the conscious mind usually does not participate during the experience, we engage it largely through memory. In passive fantasy the conscious mind is not active but functions more like a person viewing a movie or video. There is a degree of separation from the events. In active imagination ego consciousness actively engages the images and energies of the unconscious. This is intentional and deliberate, and the individual is fully awake in the experience. It is no longer a matter of watching an interesting drama "out there" on the psychic stage.

In active imagination the person jumps up onto the "stage" of the psyche and becomes involved in the unfolding story. In the written forms of active imagination it is easier to experience and define the dynamics of this process of involvement. In other forms, such as painting and dance or music, the dialogue is often more subtle, but the participant can intuit the movement of the two aspects, consciousness and the unconscious, as they interact with each other through the medium. It is also important to understand that the encounter with the images is meant to be an encounter between equals who engage one another, to explore, discuss, disagree, negotiate, argue, seek compromise, and to work things out. The dialogue is between equals; no one, no God or wisdom figure, or parent, or bombastic warrior, or threatening critic has the upper hand. The ego is not present to rule or control, but to listen, to participate, and to consider how this experience will best influence our outer lives.

This distinction of active ego involvement is of the utmost importance to the experience. It is the key to understanding the benefit of the entire exercise. Jung and various writers stress that there can be no real change and transformation through this process unless the ego takes its active role. Otherwise we are back watching an interesting film or a play up on the stage. Another way to look at this is to see that the movement from passive to active involvement of the ego is parallel with the individual moving from childhood to adulthood in terms of one's own capacity for change. It involves taking authority in and for one's own life. The dream will offer many insights, but the experiences in active imagination invites us into encounters that open us up more deeply to change.

Active ego conscious involvement, then, is what distinguishes active imagination from other meditative and fantasy activities, and this active stance of the ego contributes greatly to the capacity for transformation of the personality. Our attentiveness signals to the unconscious that we take the process seriously and that we are assigning a value of absolute reality to the unconscious realm and all that is spoken or shared.

As an aside to this point it is important for the individual to be present in the dialogic encounter as oneself, that is, as one's own ego consciousness. When I enter this realm, I do so as George and do not present myself as any other. I, George, am the one who enters the dialogue to learn, or to be given insight, to challenge and to be affirmed and affirm. To split from myself at this point may well weaken the ego's responsible role and could actually risk a destabilising psychological experience. What seems sure is that I will not receive the benefit for which I have entered, if I am not present as myself.

The second essential distinction between active imagination and other meditative practices has to do with outside influences. It is important in the active imagination encounter that the person engages only her or his own images and does not introduce any external images or influences. It is a process in which we let the unconscious speak freely through the images rather than intro-ducing a preconceived framework, structure or person that may well contaminate the encounter and weaken the opportunity for the other to speak as is appropriate and necessary. In engaging the unconscious images in active imagination we attempt to set aside any other framework. We refer to no resources except those within the situation, and simply engage whatever emerges from within.

This matter deserves some careful consideration. Louisa chose a landscape for the encounter, but the garden where afternoon tea was held was from her own dream. Therefore it was from her internal imagery. Repetitive dialogues located in previously known external landscapes, may also function as internal images of meaning if they arise from the history of the individual's own soulful journey. These landscape images may well represent safe and meaningful places for the individual. In a sense they may be a person's sacred sites and in this instance act as sacred containers for the experiences. As external as these landscape images may be in the person's history, they may also have become places of meaning in the soul's journey, and will not interfere with, but enhance the process of the encounter. To employ a safe and comfortable land- scape as the setting for a dialogue often allows the individual to enter the experience with greater confidence. We will see the use of safe and meaningful places in experiences shared in this study.

Images and frameworks that can be problematic as external influences are often religious in nature, wherein dogma, creedal belief or preconceived notions of sacred images can shape or circumscribe the content of the encounters. Likewise cultural and familial values can interfere with the open and honest pres- entation of images. Our dialogues with those within may from time to time develop in unconventional, unexpected and even off putting ways. An essential value of active imagination is that those who come will offer ideas, insights and challenges that take us outside our formerly held world view. If all they do is tell us what we already know and believe, of what value is this? To contain our conversations in the frame of our present worldview is to risk missing the new ideas and insights that may well be the catalyst for our transformation and healing. An essential function of active imagination is to bring the new, the unexplored, the previously unknown, and even the unthinkable to our conscious attention.

There is a further digression in this matter to consider here. In a Christian framework, Morton Kelsey made a significant contribution to using a variation on active imagination in his work with others and in his writing. His major written contribution is *The Other Side of Silence*. In conversations we shared many years ago, Morton took exception with the way in which active imagination was presented in Jungian circles in that it presents the notion that the encounters with the other or others will be enough to generate the healing process, even if the images were difficult or deeply disturbing. The necessary healing from the encounter would begin naturally. Kelsey felt this was a naïve attitude, especially when the individual was confronted with the forces of evil. The confrontation with evil was his major concern here. He advised that the person be able and ready to call in the Christ or another saving figure to protect one from being overwhelmed by evil forces. He separated his work in this area from Jung's by using the term image meditation. Kelsey took this imagination experience very seriously and also took the presence of evil in human life seriously. The introduction of a healing person, or a saving figure, to protect one from evil in the dialogic encounter was essential to Kelsey's understanding of this work.

In my own active imagination work there have been times when I have engaged interior characters on my own that were frightening, and at times I have invited the Christ figure to be with me. This Christ figure, for me, is a distinct internal character built upon the traditions of my long association with my faith and cultural worlds. The Christ image for me has both external origins, and a distinct internal character and integrity that correspond to my personal needs at any time. It seems to me that the essential issue here is to allow the images from the unconscious the freedom to speak as they desire and to trust ourselves to know when to call upon an internal wisdom figure to stand with us in instances when there is a sense of threat. In my own experience the matter has been further complicated by the conclusion that the harder path is often a better choice for me than the easy one. We will see consider this Christ figure again in chapter five as an example of sacred images in active imagination. This may be one of those reflections has an no end point.

By way of summary, then, active imagination is a meditation process, a creative method of engaging the unconscious, most often by using images, but also at times by using movement, sound or artistic expression. The goal is to connect actively, from the standpoint of ego consciousness, with the unconscious life, through the symbolic images. It is important to affirm that the experience of active imagination encompasses a wide variety of practices that can be interpreted in different ways. It is also important to consider carefully how to give the inner figures the freedom to present whatever it is they have come to share with our conscious minds and not to be confined in preconceived imagery or attitudes.

When?

A common question concerning the practice of active imagination is *when* we might use the experience. When is it appropriate to use this practice? Most people come to the experience seeking a way to address a time of conscious crisis. We engage the dialogue to create a conversation between ego consciousness and that part of us who feels the pain of the crisis. The dialogue gives us a way of listening to our own different voices and opinions as we seek a way forward to resolution or action. Active imagination provides us with a sense of inner space between ego consciousness and that part of us that is stressed. The dialogue allows us to create objectivity between consciousness and the other within so that we do not feel overwhelmed by whatever is the issue at the time. The helpful language tool here is "part of me." In our dialogues we are able to move from "I am angry," to "part of me is angry." The space between consciousness and our anger allows us to realise that part of me is *not* angry, and I can seek through a dialogue to understand consciously what is the issue and how to work for resolution. In the introductory case material, Louisa was not only confronting difficult challenges on the outside, her inner responses were conflicted and this made decision making a difficult process. It was an appropriate time to employ active imagination and to give voice to those inner persons who held such a diversity of opinions on the present circumstance.

In terms of crisis experiences, active imagination is a way for individuals feeling stuck in life to engage with the person, or persons, within who seem unable to change, or who block the way forward and want to remain in old ways of being and thinking. It is a way to get different points of view in one's thinking to work together toward some middle ground or forward resolution. A person who is anxious or depressed can use active imagination to seek insight into underlying causes. The process of dialogue with whatever part of us that is distressed may offer new ways to come to resolution, reconciliation and healing.

Most of us have known the experience of being at odds with ourselves over some matter. John O'Donohue, in his work *Anam Cara*, compares this experience to an inner feud, and for many people these conflicts within are like living in a war zone. A central task of active imagination is to end the civil war, to use the dialogues to seek peace and reconciliation between conflicted points of view. Often the dialogues can enable a coming together of the parts of us that have been in conflict for a very long time. In this dialogic practice the individual can engage different perspectives and voices of opposition, as Louisa did in her dialogues. Active imagination becomes a way to work to resolve the crises that emerge frequently when our limited conscious point of view encounters strongly felt, and sometimes dramatically, diverse opinions. Active imagination increases our capacity to engage our internal differences, and to open us to the richness of our natural complexity.

Years ago a friend told me that he was considering a major move to another part of his state. He consulted the villagers as to how they saw the idea and came away with a greater confidence in his plan. He told me that he would now not make any major decision until he ran the idea by the villagers. My friend's experience invites us to affirm that, in addition to times of crisis, active imagination can also be a time to reflect with our soul family on new opportunities that emerge. As my friend did, we can listen to the villagers express their points of view over a house move, a move to a different city, the possibility of taking up advanced study, a new hobby, or deciding to enter more deeply into a relationship. It can be very grounding to hear the voices of those within offer their counsel, caution and/or support as we contemplate stepping into something new. It is a simple reminder that "we," all of us, are in life's adventures together.

As we look at the practice, it is interesting to realise that active imagination may not be a foreign experience for most of us. It seems that many of us have out loud moments of conversation or comment with ourselves. Some of these moments are quite spontaneous, and others may be a natural reflective way to think about matters at hand. For some this may have a playful character, much like the imaginary playmates of childhood. When I introduced the possibility of this experience to a client some years ago, he acknowledged that he had been using the process for some time without knowing anything about it as an identifiable practice. On an amusing note, Mary Watkins, in her work, *Invisible Guests*, believes that we never stop the dialogues that begin quite naturally in childhood. She wonders with whom we are speaking when we stub a toe on the concrete sidewalk as we move down the street, and begin unconsciously to comment on the experience.

In terms of its purpose and appropriate use, active imagination is a process we use *when* we seek engagement, dialogue and encounter between aspects of our souls that are mysterious and puzzling, *when* we are polarised and in conflict with a variety of points of view, and *when* we desire to reflect on new and creative opportunities and changes. We can use it to explore feelings of depression and anxiety, anger and rage or any significant feeling response to life. We can employ the practice in those times when we feel indecisive and unsure of how to go forward in life. It is an activity the energy of which functions to give insight and clarity, and to integrate, encourage, bring resolution, reconcile and to end the inner conflicts that so often rumble away in our souls. We seek to befriend those we first experienced as enemies and ground ourselves in a more contented inner life.

The process

Having defined active imagination, and having considered briefly when a person might use it, we now look at the process itself. The focus here is primarily on written active imagination, which seems to be the most common way to engage the experience. The process I describe here has grown out of my own experience and the experiences of people with whom I have worked for more than thirty-five years. In actual practice each person will make variations on the general process according to individual need and temperament. I still hand write my dialogue experiences, some others use the computer or phone. While there are important essential aspects of the practice, we each will create a process that suits us.

As with any meditation experience, preparation is simple and it is important. In a sense our preparation gives focus and embodies our intention. It is important to choose a comfortable setting, usually indoors, for the experience. It is best that it is a place where it is possible to be alone with no concern for interruptions. It is advisable to create the space away from the phone and any other electronic devices unless "writing" on one. A space of solitude eliminates having to worry about other people interrupting while we write, or dance, sing, compose, model or paint. Often what we produce is not for the eyes of others at this stage, if ever. In such instances wherein I have been invited by an inner figure to dance to a chant, it has been essential for me to be alone otherwise I would have been too self-conscious to get up from my chair. The setting also needs to be comfortable in terms of temperature. Any space that is too cold or too hot may be distracting. Active imagination, like most meditative exercises, is an altered state of consciousness in which the bodily functions relax and slow down. Spaces that are too warm cause me to get sleepy; in cold places I get concerned about my physical discomfort.

By stressing a solitary, indoor place, I do not want to rule out the possibility of engaging in this experience out of doors. Weather and circumstances permitting, this can work well as a variation. In certain circumstances I have found it very easy to experience active imagination by the ocean. The timeless rhythm of the waves almost always assists me in the settling down process.

Likewise, I have had significant experiences on a very large rock by a mountain stream that was long a favourite and sacred place for me. Overall, if I am too close to the activities of other people and their voices, I find it hard to settle down and focus on my experience.

As with any meditative experience I have found it important to assist the settling down by paying attention to my posture and to my breathing. Most often when I am in a room I sit comfortably in a straight chair at a table with both feet squarely on the floor and my back relaxed but straight. In the out of doors I situate myself comfortably on a rock or on the sand in such a position that I am able to write, and avoid any cramping. I begin with some deep breathing to help settle me, and then let my breathing take its own pace. For a while I may close my eyes and allow myself to pause for a time as I relax.

It is also necessary to choose beforehand the method and medium for the experience. Here I am focused on writing. It's important to organise paper, or journal, pencil or pen, the computer or phone, and a surface on which to work. Likewise, if another medium, such as painting, is chosen, supplies need to be arranged adequately in advance. We need also to make sure that our setting allows adequate space for our chosen medium. It is disorienting to begin this kind of encounter with the unconscious, and then not to be able to respond spontaneously due to lack of preparation.

These initial steps in settling down assist us in suspending the rational, critical function of the mind. For most of us this is not easy. Here we set aside the rational part of us by intention as best we can. We begin here with trust in the integrity of what awaits as we engage the unconscious in its native language of poetic imagery. This trust allows us to approach the images with openness and move into the realm of soul. For me, it is to enter the psychic world of myth and symbol, that vital and vibrant life-stream that runs continually beneath the surface of my life's chronological activities.

The process is a kind of emptying exercise that creates space for the images of the unconscious to engage our conscious attention. It means taking the risk of relaxing our control of our conscious minds and being open to whatever will come into our awareness. For many of us this is a difficult challenge partly because of our cultural training. Most of us have been well schooled to be reasonable, rational and to value highly self-control. In my experience self-control is equated with maturity and essential to success in our culture. In the practice of active imagination we set aside this dominant cultural teaching and choose to enter the domain of myth, symbol, the poetic, the imprecise, mystery, the domain of soul. To engage this practice is a substantial challenge. Often our intention triggers anxiety in our conscious minds over the issue of control. It is not unusual for this anxiety to manifest quickly as fear and dismissal. Most of us fear the unknown depths of our souls, and our rational selves can accuse us of making things up, for the images which appear and challenge us "could not possibly be real." On countless occasions people have presented a first experience of active imagination and then dismissed it as useless or of no value. The rational part of us often struggles with our engagement with the deeper, mysterious realms of our soul. This first step is a substantial challenge, and many of us only undertake it when we are driven to realise we have run out of options to understand ourselves, our puzzling reactions to others, our own surprising feelings and our startling dreams for our future.

Several years ago I had an amusing initial experience that symbolises the suspension of the function of my rational, critical mind. It is an image to which I still turn whenever I am having trouble settling down. In the image I sit next to an old, silent monk, who appeared in my internal world many years ago, and who almost never speaks. After I sit with him for a while, he leans over, opens my head as if it is hinged, removes my brain, and closes my head again. With this symbolic action I am then free to begin the dialogue experience.

Once we have settled into our quiet place, we can sense that the time is right to begin. For me, the starting place is often an image from a dream or fantasy, or the need to speak with an inner figure, someone new or an old friend from the village. Sometimes I have no image. It may simply be a mood, feeling, or issue. In this instance I address what I name as the "abyss," and ask the mood, energy or issue of concern to take a form to which I can relate so that we may talk with each other. It is inviting the unconscious into the dialogue.

Here again I affirm the importance of not using outside references for images unless they are already a significant image in the inner world. Specifically here it is important to separate an inner figure from someone whom we know in our outer lives. Both Barbara Hannah and Robert Johnson in their works cited earlier stress the importance of this principle. Separating outer and inner figures at this point protects both from constriction, confusion and contamination. It has been my practice when a person known to me appears in a dream with whom I then decide to dialogue, to negotiate first a name change. This frees the inner character to develop on its own, and respects the outer person as an individual in her or his own right, and as one separate from our projections. I tend to ask the image for the name by which it desires to be known in an attempt to show respect and to give the image agency in the dialogue. There are times when we may want to rehearse a conversation with someone whom we know in our outer lives. This has potential to be a valuable process in working toward resolution and reconciliation. I sense that it is different to active imagination as we explore it here.

As we become quiet and pay close attention, we remain focused on the original image that presents itself. As I have affirmed, active imagination is not free association wherein one builds out and away from an original image with subsequent images. It is direct association with the original image. If more than one image is present, we move our focus from one to another slowly so as to remain actively focused in the process, and not risk falling into a more passive fantasy process where we again simply observe what is going on and not engage with the images directly.

We are to remain active from the outset. Most always it is the original image that contains the insight or answer to our dilemma or crisis, and we need to work with it, even if it seems strange, silly or frightening. What animates the image in the first instance is our attentive focus. As we remain focused on it, the image most often will take on life, so to speak, and will respond to our attempt to engage it. It is as if we breathe life into the images simply by being attentive to them. In those rare instances when the images refuse to speak, it has become my usual response to suggest patience and indicate a willingness to wait, and to return again and again until the image is ready to speak. It is possible the waiting is part of the healing or solution. If after a time we feel impatient at the continued silence, it may well be appropriate to express our impatience with the process, and to challenge the image to speak. This, too, may well be a part of the desired response that will lead to healing. In making decisions about our initial responses there is no simple, single solution. Our judgements must be made in the context of the experience. I remember one woman who approached a male figure, who was seated facing away from her like a stone statue. She had to return and seek to engage him four times before he chose to speak. Her persistence provided the necessary evidence that she was serious in her pursuit of some form of relationship. The experience also challenged her to find her voice and to persevere with her opinions and desires in the outer world as well.

Whether we enter the process with an image from a dream or another source, or the image emerges in response to our focused attention on the abyss, once we have a clear sense of that image, we are ready to proceed. If working with a visual form we begin to paint or draw, or with our bodies to sing or dance freely, with no concern for how it all might appear to others. What matters is that we suspend our judgement and allow the process to unfold spontaneously. If we are engaging in dialogue, we enter that process by taking up the first exchange. I usually try to begin with a question, as this keeps me focused on the image and invites the image to respond.

The mechanics of recording a dialogue process bears some attention. In my earlier experiences I engaged the characters spontaneously, and let the story unfold while sitting in my chair. Often there was narrative movement as well as dialogue. Immediately after the experience I would record the exchange in my journal, and recall whatever I could remember of the dialogue and action. I soon realised that I was missing much of the experience, and perhaps conveniently forgetting many important details and exchanges. I then took up recording the experience as it happened. I was writing the dialogue like a play script with parentheses around narrative actions amid the exchanges. At first this scribing process seemed clumsy to me, but now it has become my preferred form. I note the rather convenient fact that the dialogue exchanges tend to keep pace with the speed of my writing.

Again, spontaneity is the key to the process. We need to let the material come forward without censorship. It is important to resist the natural tendency to edit the language and to insert the proper punctuation as we go along, as if we were creating a great literary art form. To dress up the written record as it unfolds is to risk losing the raw honesty of the encounter. We need to let the images speak honestly. What emerges is only for us in this original form, so it can be as rough, rude, incoherent, beautiful and creative as it needs to be as it arises spontaneously from the unconscious.

In my personal practice the dialogue is recorded as a play script. One variation that a colleague has used is to type the conversation running together, using the upper case letters for the inner voice and the lower case letters for her own responses. Another colleague told of another variation on the scripted recording. When speaking with a child, she used her preferred hand for her own voice and her other hand for the voice of the child. It seemed to have a positive effect on the child's expression, that is, to speak as a child rather than as a little adult. Right after the experience, I find it useful to go back through the play script dialogue and indicate in the margin who is speaking which lines, and check to make sure the narrative sections are in parentheses for clarity.

In the dialogue it is important to remain focused and to listen, even if what emerges is unpleasant or shocking to our conscious minds. Often, as we begin to engage the unconscious, the early material is confronting and upsetting. As we begin to explore the inner life our early encounters are often with the shadow side of our personality, that energy that stands opposite to our conscious, chosen persona. Most of us are continually surprised to learn that the opposite of all we have tried to be still travels with us. The inner dialogue or creative process demands courage in order to continue with those we meet and from whom we learn more about our complete selves.

The starting place for my first long series of active imagination dialogues was a dream about a Great Dane dog that met me at the entrance to an old dark house, barking loudly. I was frightened, my way in seemed blocked, so I left and returned to my car. As I sat in the driver's seat, a man rose up out of the back seat and put a gun to my head. Being sensible, I woke up! It was at the encouragement of my analyst at the time that I took up a dialogue approach to the disturbing dream of the barking dog. Some days after the dream, in active imagination, I approached the house with some care. For me, at my height, Great Dane dogs are what we might call an "eye level" experience! When I got to the entry door and pushed it open, the dog again came bounding and barking down the hall to scare me off. Here I changed the dream story in the active imagination process and stood my ground. I yelled back at the barking dog and told him to stop. I then told the dog I wanted to enter the house. He responded quickly with a surprising question. Dog asked, "Are you serious about this?" I was surprised and somewhat shaken at being confronted with this question. After a hesitation I answered, "Yes." I may have added, "I think I am." The dog stood aside and I entered the house, and was told to follow along behind.

That open door led to extraordinary experiences of my own inner world over the next two years, and these experiences resulted in new self-understanding, deep and lasting healing, and an enriched inner life. It all began with the challenge: "Are you serious about this?" It is important to begin active imagi-nation with serious resolve, and to be prepared with courage to engage whatever meets us eye to eye. I have come to conclude, based on my experience and that of others over the years, that the entrance into active imagination may well include an initiation process that tests our serious intent. It is of the same theme as that experienced by the woman mentioned earlier who had to approach the silent man four times and with some impatience to get a response.

It is also important to remember again that the process is a dialogue. As I have stated previously, it is meant to be a two-way exchange, a dialogue between equals. Several years ago I saw a woman for inner work for a short period of time. During this time she presented active imagination dialogues with a male figure. In their conversations he was rude, unpleasant and demeaning to her. I suggested that she stand up to him and disagree with his perspective, or even risk telling him off. She could not bring herself to do this. For her it was not appropriate to challenge the inner male figure. In her outer life she was really stuck, and it had to do largely with the men in her life. I could see why. She was stuck on the inside because she would not dialogue with this inner man who berated her, she just stood there and took it, and she remained stuck on the outside because of it. Active imagination involves dialogue, interaction, and sometimes very heated and dramatic exchanges. We are in dialogue with parts of ourselves, and attempting to create together a new and more wholesome life. This cannot happen if we attribute some kind of awesome infallibility to the other within and never challenge or question what is presented to us.

In the dialogue, then, it is important to ask questions, to disagree, to argue. We come together in the inner dialogue process as equals. No one in the dialogue is custodian of the complete truth, and our task from the standpoint of ego consciousness is to engage the inner figures in order to learn together what a more complete truth might be for lives, both inner and outer.

A part of honest dialogue may well be the stirring up of intense emotions. Active imagination happens in the symbolic realm of soul and is not simply a cerebral exercise. A man who worked with me for several years had a most surprising experience when he first encountered a shadow-like figure. He had not written out a dialogue, so he decided to stand and talk to the shadow-like figure in my office. He was agitated as he began; he was impatient with this shadowy one who would not appear clearly and speak. His voice became very loud and suddenly he started striking the air, trying to hit at the mysterious one who was there but silent. He became very angry, and was intensely involved. It was to no avail for the other within was not prepared to speak at that time. While the experience did not result in any satisfactory dialogic exchange, through his embodied experience, he became convinced of the importance of what he was doing, and went on to pursue an encounter with this mysterious inner figure in different ways.

Yet another man brought amazing dialogues with one, and then two, young boys for us to review. He had been slow to come to this method, but when he risked using it, the results were very helpful. The accounts with the boys that he shared were quite amazing. The man was inspired, and revealed the native talents of a grand storyteller. In reviewing his dialogues with me, he read the parts of the dialogues with great emotion and character, even moving around in his chair as he addressed the others. The dialogues were as insightful as they were delightful, and I would propose they opened to this man a whole new dimension of his emotional life as well as giving him insight into his spiritual journey and the issues he needed to address. It is important to enter the active imagination process fully and to be prepared to experience it with the full range of our emotions.

Another important consideration in this process is with our overall values. In the dialogue experiences a variety of points of view may well emerge. This is in fact the point of the exercise. It is the job of consciousness to take the ethical stance in the proceedings and to hold to our present ethical perspective. Sometimes attitudes or suggestions for action will go against the values of our conscious lives and our culture. It is up to consciousness to carry the ethical concern in the process. Blind obedience to the unconscious disregards the essential nature of active imagination. The overall function of the inner figures, however they express their perspective, is to balance our conscious point of view, and to enrich our lives. The process is centred in compensation and balance, aimed at harmony, not domination by an unconscious energy that may well have no regard for the values of our daily lives. The tasks of ego consciousness in this regard are to hold our ground with values that are of importance to us, to refuse to allow any inner character to take over and manipulate us to act in contradiction to our grounded values, and to consider, in dialogue, ways to integrate effectively any new points of view into our daily living. At the same time the values we have held consciously may be challenged strongly, and we may need to amend our present stance in order to live peacefully with the new aspects of ourselves that emerge through our dialogues.

To conclude with the mechanics of the process, we stay with the encounter until a sense of resolution or completion emerges. Once we become accustomed to these experiences we come to trust the timing and flow of the encounters. Usually they begin with an issue or the statement of a problem, continue with a dialogue or other activity of engagement, in which various points of view are presented, and end with some sense of completion, at least for the time being.

It has become my practice to end the experience with some moment of reflection. This might include gratitude for the experience. Most often I simply speak aloud. Hearing my own voice acts to assist me in making the return from the psychic realm of imagination, and to reconnect with my present outer time and place. Occasionally this process takes a little time. It is important not to rush, but to take our time and make the transition a gentle one.

As I affirmed at the outset of this description of the process of active imagination, any description must be very general; variations on the basic experience will differ widely. What matters is the goal. It is to make contact with the unconscious energies and images that are a great source of wisdom and insight and who very often assist us in broadening our lives toward a greater wholeness.

Once we have completed an active imagination exercise, it seems wise to consider choosing an action as a way to honour the experience and to integrate it more into our conscious world. Robert Johnson, in *Inner Work*, suggests that we use a ritual action to make the connection. It can be a simple one and does not need to include the one or ones with whom we have had dialogue, what matters is that we make the connection in our minds between the dialogue experience and the ritual. A ritual act that has been helpful to me is to read my dialogues aloud during my times of devotion. It is quite moving to hear the dialogues spoken into the room, to hear them through my hearing and not just in my interior mental processes. They tend to become more alive and the meaning more clear. The ritual act underscores that these dialogues, along with our dreams, are our personal sacred texts, the rich source of wisdom from the depths of the soul. Rarely will the texts look anything like the sacred writings of a religious tradition, but they are ours, intimate and deeply meaningful texts that bring insight and encourage us toward our wholeness.

In this first chapter we have defined active imagination and considered the actual process in the written form of the experience. We now turn our attention to matters relating to our experiences and to some of the benefits that come from our adventures into the realm of dialogue with soul figures.

CHAPTER TWO

Relating to the Experience

We cannot change anything unless we accept it.
Condemnation does not liberate, it oppresses.
Carl Jung

Having engaged the symbolic and mythical world of active imagination, there are several matters to consider as we learn to live with, and learn from, the experiences. The first is to affirm again that this is not an art form. My focus here is on written texts in these reflections, but I suggest that much of this will apply to other forms of expression as well. In regard to writing, what we want from the experience is the simple, raw and unedited text. Our intention is give the "others" in our souls the right and privilege to speak as they choose. We strive to keep the process as spontaneous as possible and not tidy up the text as we go. It is tempting, perhaps for most of us, to want to create a finished product. We can easily be led astray from the creative encounter with concerns for form, punctuation, conventional expressions and judgements. The first step in relating to the experience is to leave the text alone and engage it as it has come forward. In the experience and immediately after, concerns for commas can lead us away from the impact and meaning of the experience.

Also we need to resist our inclinations to seek quickly an understanding through intellectual analysis and interpretation using some system or construct. This risks flattening the symbols and draining the energy from the experience. What may have been numinous for us could quickly be rendered ordinary and dull. To interpret a text too quickly can contaminate the spontaneous flow of subsequent dialogues with preconceived notions as to how things "should" unfold.

A deeper challenge here is to acknowledge that we are not only rational beings but also mythical persons. In an age when rational thinking is highly prized, and we are encouraged at every turn to have answers and to be reasonable, it takes great effort to let the interior mythic dialogues and stories remain as they have come. It is a challenge to live quietly with them, the stories, the insights, the energy of the characters, and the sense of benefit stirring in us. We are challenged to realise and affirm that we can receive great benefit from our imagined, symbolic experiences even if we do not fully understand them.

In dealing with active imagination material then, the primary value resides in having the experience itself, and secondarily, in how we understand and respond to it. Like most creative, poetic and artistic endeavours, active imagination brings us into relationship with the realm of the inexhaustible, the realm of mystery. The entire exercise requires a respect for this realm of mystery, and the recognition that we can benefit greatly from these active imagination experiences, the complete meaning of which we may never grasp.

Holding the experiences

Some years ago a friend rang me to tell me that a friend of his was visiting from overseas. He had told her about my work and she expressed an interest in meeting me. We set a time to meet and in that conversation we spoke at length about active imagination. This included using the image of a village to act as the container for the characters we meet. Several days later she sent me a reflection on the various people who she intuited were part of her interior world. Here is the reflection.

The Village of Smith

The village of Smith stands in desert country, but it has been watered and cared for, and now there are trees and flowers and grass. The owners are rather like Bedouin – they like colour, style and passion – but the terrain forces a basic sort of simplicity, even austerity, which they also have a taste for.

The desert has its *hermit*, who loves the solitude, the remoteness, the stars. The other villagers are a bit nervous of the hermit, though, that her reclusive life-style might somehow get forced on them.

Chief worrier is *Ms. Gregarious* who loves people, bustle and chatter, feels that is the way to stay "normal."

Fears of not being normal are strong in the village because of the weirdness of a kind of *prophet* character who has from time to time had a lot of experience they would class as "mad." She does not think so – she thinks they are a way to a new sort of understanding – but she knows there are dangers around that stuff. She feels if she could get their help and support she could let herself have the experiences and generally move on. But they – the neighbours – don't give her much confidence.

The *One who has a speech impediment* is close to the prophet and probably sympathises with her, but is a pretty detached character – a truth-teller, a Cassandra, who tells truths nobody wants to know. But incorruptible.

The *blacksmith* is the maker and creator of the village, and the strongest person in it. He is about the same task as the prophet, but on different lines – taking material out of the depths and shaping it or using it for the general good.

The *child*, orphaned young, who has a huge need to be taken care of, but is afraid if someone does take care of her, they will go off her, or become possessive.

The *feckless* person – Irish – who, like the child, hopes/expects to be taken care of. But good at living in the moment. Selfish in a devious way.

The *friend*. One of the more relaxed characters in the place. Receives a lot of happiness and maybe gives it, at least some.

The *respectable lady*. Ready to vanish into conformity on occasion. Dreads adventure, change and new things.

The *lover* – fairly adventurous but makes bad choices, gives too much, loses sight of boundaries. Likes sex a lot or hates it. Frightened to death of rejection.

Maternal woman – very strong. Likes helping younger women and men and often does seem able to make them happier. General pleasure in caring for people, which tho' deriving from cheering up the orphaned child, still seems useful and enjoyable.

The *failure*. Need not be too successful or to earn too much money as that feels dangerous.

The *ambitious woman*. Loathes the Failure and curses her (him?).

I do not know what further use this woman made of her reflection because she returned home and we had no further contact. While we do not know what came next for her, we can see that her initial response was to give spontaneous shape to a diverse group of characters that lived in her village. The complexity of her interior world emerged easily in this form. In this exercise alone there is potential benefit. Regardless of whatever followed, this exercise opened up creative pathways to a deeper wholeness.

I have mentioned the village previously, and as we engage here with benefits from the active imagination experience, I want to highlight this image. The village is, for me, a positive container in which to gather the characters from our active imagination experiences.

The village image is my way of creating, or discovering, an inner "place" in which the various people live. It functions as a safe container to hold the complex characters who make up my psychic world. It provides a coherent psychic vessel to hold together the sometimes wildly different people who present themselves in my active imagination encounters.

The village of Smith is in desert country, yet not barren. Care has been given and there is vegetation. Those who lived in this place are like Bedouin, fond of colour, style and passion. It is an austere landscape but one with character. It is interesting to wonder what this landscape meant for this woman since it is foreign to her country of origin. Perhaps our interior landscapes seek to promote our wholeness through compensation with an entirely different frame from the one in which we usually live.

The image of my village has grown in detail over many years. It is off in a forested area and is accessible only through a narrow opening in a rock face. A walking path goes past that rock face and it would be easy to miss the opening. Passing through the narrow opening I come to a village of huts that are arranged in a circle. All are facing in to a centre courtyard, a gathering place, in the middle of which stands a tall tree. A low wall of stone surrounds the gathering area that also serves as a sitting bench. Looking out over the wall in one direction I can see the deep valley, and in another direction I see a hillside with a path up the incline leading to a higher vantage point. The various villagers live in the huts, they use the centre courtyard for their gathering times. Once I enter through the narrow gap in the rock face I come to the first hut that is the home of the Wise Old Man. He is like a gatekeeper. The ritual of entry is to stop and greet him and be welcomed by him. I often state my concern or state of mind and he sends me out the other door of his hut into the centre circle. My departure is to return through his hut and offer thanks and farewell. These are long-standing rituals of reverence for entering and leaving. This describes something of my village container.

A friend who undertook this work some years ago found himself with his villagers in a forest clearing gathered around a campfire that later was relocated at the foot of a high mountain shrouded in cloud. It was the mountain of God. The cloud often drifted down from the mountain to the gathering below as a form of blessing. The gathering place for another young man was a village square with stone benches around a central tree. Here he sat on the bench to speak with whoever came forward. Each image is different for us, sometimes it is chosen by us and sometimes it seems to emerge from within of its own accord. It is interesting to note the role of nature for many in the image of the village. The village image acts as a grounded "place" for the various people to gather who become the meaningful and vibrant characters of our interior mythic life. The use of a place image provides a stable foundation for the coming together of the various parts of us who become a diverse family of sub-personalities to our consciousness. We have in the village the benefit of an image that is an intimate and significant frame in which to hold together the complex characters that make up our lives.

Benefits of Active Imagination

As we engage active imagination as part of our soul work, we receive several benefits over time from our experiences. The *first* benefit involves a growing self-understanding. The active imagination exercise has the immediate effect of expanding our conscious awareness, specifically our conscious self-concept. By engaging these others within, we get to know diverse aspects of ourselves that we wouldn't admit to ordinarily, or that we wouldn't have dreamed were characters within the realm of who we might become. The process of extending our conscious boundaries is a simple, enriching experience.

Expanding of our consciousness through the experience of active imagination helps us to relate to ourselves in a new way. Inner dialogues help us realise that we are really many selves rather than one self. Some have referred to these selves as a multitude, or a crowd, or even a zoo. The village image works best for me. Our mental health requires a strong ego-conscious self, this strong sense of self can be strengthened when we realise that our deeper self actually seems to be made up of a village, or multitude, or crowd of people who represent different points of view, and who sometimes conflict with each other in their perspectives. Robust conversations in the village can actually help us engage life in more honest and grounded interactions.

In trying to explain this in workshops, I used a simple "show and tell" method. I held up a single sheet of paper from the copy machine and suggested that this represented our conscious self-understanding without reference to the unconscious or the practice of active imagination. I then held up nine sheets of paper taped together to demonstrate the expansion of our conscious self-understanding when we engaged the unconscious images through active imagination. The visual contrast made the point.

One of the word maps that is helpful to me and that I have offered to others in this context is to speak of "part of me." Rather than saying, "I am angry," we say, "part of me is angry." This allows us to recognise that we are able to have very different and simultaneous feeling reactions to any given situation. Part of me faces change with fear and hesitation; part of me embraces change with excitement and a sense of adventure. Often I have more than one reaction to the circumstances and events that emerge in life. The "part of me" tool helps us get comfortable with our complexity, especially in the face of a dominant culture that seems still to want things to divide easily into either/or categories. More often life is part of me this and part of me that. The village helps us hold and contain our complex responses to our ongoing lives. The dialogue practice allows us to have conversation with various parts of us that are involved in any given experience. Through our practice we can work toward collaboration and resolution, rather than expending our energy in internal conflict.

Our practice also creates a certain sense of objectivity or distance between my consciousness and other villagers. It creates a sense of space between me and me. Once I realise that only part of me is angry, I am less susceptible to being overwhelmed by my anger. I realise that part of me is angry, and other parts of me may well have other and very different responses to the matter at hand.

This practice of dialoguing with parts of us supports our commitment to making friends with ourselves and to welcoming all into the village. We recognise that even those who appear hostile and adversarial have something to say, something to teach our limited consciousness. The core truth and principle here is *radical inclusivity*. Rather than seeking maturity or perfection by getting rid of difficult, frightening or distasteful parts of ourselves, we welcome them in, realising that each has something of value to contribute to our wholeness. Engaging over time with everyone in the village, we are able to open to a more complete, whole sense of ourselves. We need to remember that what we push away does not go away. Those parts of us we try to annihilate or ignore only sink back into the shadows of the unconscious. They will respond then with guerrilla warfare tactics and look for times to surprise us with eruptions into the outer world that cause us difficulty, shame or serious trouble. Over the years, whoever emerges in the soul's journey is in, like it or not. Active imagination offers us a way to encounter these troublesome ones, the forgotten ones, the hidden ones, and negotiate a more inclusive way to be together. What we are working toward here is self-love. The village image serves as a safe container in which these challenging others learn to live along with the rest of us. We relate through encounter, engagement and dialogue, and we offer them hospitality in our village to remain internally part of who we are.

If we can and will expand our conscious boundaries by beginning to see ourselves more as a family or village than as a simple, singular self, we will be able to cope more easily with the conflicts and ambivalent feelings so common to us in our daily living. The "part of me" tool helps us determine with more confidence and serenity how we feel, think or want to react to certain relationships and situations. As we become aware of this way of relating to ourselves we are also able to look at who's talking when a specific mood, opinion or feeling emerges. This is particularly helpful if what emerges is in conflict with the values and principles we normally hold. Such a practice enables us more quickly and easily to come to terms with ourselves in all our myriad and varied feelings, attitudes, moods and opinions. This expanding self-consciousness will bring us a deeper sense of peace.

Somewhere along the journey I realised that if I tie a string with a ball on the end to another cord pulled taught, the ball could only go as high as it goes low. The point this makes for me is that I can only go as high as I am willing to go low in life. If this is so, then, in the inner journey, if we refuse to engage the mysterious, frightening, troublesome and adventuresome depths of our own souls, we constrict the possibilities of seeing the blessings, the wonders and joys of our lives. Expanding our conscious boundaries, coming to know ourselves more fully, means engaging both the images of darkness and of light within us. This first benefit of active imagination requires of us the courage to face the difficult aspects of our souls, so that we may also experience more fully our positive qualities and moments as well.

The *second* benefit of active imagination involves the gradual diminishing of the dominant influence of the unconscious. This practice will bring to light much that has been unconscious, and can help us understand more clearly and quickly when we are projecting our own inner agenda or needs onto others. Years ago I heard a speaker observe that much of life is about withdrawing projections. It is a natural, pre-rational, spontaneous process. While active imagination will not eliminate this natural projection process, it does reduce the dangers involved by helping our consciousness connect with inner contents more quickly. This means that we, and others, will be less the victims of our unconscious projections. In a sense the practice will help the ego remain more flexible in relating to others by helping us see that many of our relationships are tinged with projections of our own needs, desires and opinions, and our limits. Rather than falling into rigid and defensive ego postures in the face of diversity, we are more able to make room for difference, and for others who invite us to think outside the boundaries of our ordinary, daily lives.

For many of us in our ordinary conversations the phrase, "I don't know," emerges from time to time. While there are times when we do not know in fact, in this context this phrase can represent the ego's resistance to knowing. It is as if we are saying, "I don't want to know." It can be a defence against new ideas, information, opinions and insights. It is a capitulation to the dominance of the unconscious as a way of avoiding the unsettling expansion of our present conscious understanding. I will risk the guess that there are times when most of us would rather remain where we are in our worldview than to take up a new path that opens to us.

This second benefit of active imagination can help us withdraw our projections, and helps us to be less likely to fall prey to unconscious domination. It invites us to confront our conscious resistance to knowing and to risk paying the price of an expanded awareness so that we might also receive its many benefits.

The implication here is that consciousness is the primary goal of this soul work. It functions as an ethic in that conscious knowing minimises any negative impact we have on others and ourselves. Not knowing is the primary problem. The more we understand ourselves and come to terms with ourselves, the less we project our unconscious attitudes, needs and opinions onto others and the less harm we'll do. In our soul work self-awareness is highly valued, and active imagination strengthens this awareness.

Along with the expanded self-awareness that grows up in us through this practice is the realisation that the centre of our personalities shifts from being centred entirely in our conscious points of view, to a mid-point between consciousness and the unconscious. My friend who decided that he would not make any major decision until he sought the input of those in his village demonstrates this shift. Most of us have grown up in cultures that put high values on being clear and precise in knowing what to think, how to decide and what to do. In this cultural model, the centre of our personalities is our ego-consciousness supported by a clear set of values deeply influenced by the cultures of family, faith and society. Active imagination introduces to us the diverse and complex nature of who we are, and helps us realise the limits of consciousness and the depth of wisdom that resides in our complex souls. Along with this we realise that we stand apart in some instances from the values cultivated in us by our various cultures.

Active imagination shifts the centre of personality to a mid point between consciousness and the unconscious. The practice results in a shift away from the notion that our centre point is identical with ego-consciousness and results in the shaping of our worldview that is unique to us and, at times, counter-cultural in some way. Our reflection here is not meant to discount the importance of a strong ego, a strong ego is critical to our mental health. Our focus is to help us be aware of a more comprehensive sense of our selves when we say, "I am". Our experience is more that "I am," actually includes "we are," and we are in continual dialogue with the great variety of helpful and troublesome characters in the village.

Again, our internal conversations are dialogues between

equals. Once we begin the practice we realise that there are treasured points of view residing in the depths of our souls. Active imagination invites us to take the unconscious seriously and to give those in the village a chance to cooperate with consciousness instead of having to assault us to get our attention. We are making potential enemies into friends. It is collaborative, soulful living. The shift to mid-point is a radical decision to make and the result is a more cooperative, collaborative relationship with the multitudes, the crowd that we are.

The dialogue between equals means, again, that no one inner character carries the absolute authority of the God image. The dynamic is one of balance; there is give and take, disagreement and compromise. As equals, the inner characters emerge not to dominate, but to balance, to create a new vision of what it is to be us, and what it is to be a more complete human. As we encounter this inner, unconscious world through active imagination, a new sense of who "I am – we are" emerges. We are less dominated by the unconscious and, through our new self-awareness, and more cooperative with it. Paradoxically, this engagement with the unconscious actually strengthens consciousness, so that one is less likely to be caught up in the grips of the unconscious energy and its influence.

A *third* benefit of the active imagination experience is an overall change in personality. This change is a natural flow on result from the shift of the centre of one's sense of self exclusively based in consciousness, to the mid-point between consciousness and the unconscious. This change for most of us is gradual in character, and it is usually quite subtle. While usually not dramatic, for most it is a pervasive change, one that involves a transformation of our entire general attitude toward ourselves and toward life.

The change includes the recognition and acceptance that the ego is not the paramount authority in one's life. If we are to be more whole and balanced in life, ego consciousness must acknowledge a sense of dependence, or interdependence, on the unconscious and its capacity to cultivate a more wholesome sense of self. Again it is collaborating from the mid-point in the soul.

We often see these gradual changes foreshadowed in an insight from a dialogue or dream experience. It is as if the unconscious anticipates and declares what is coming. The integration of the change into our daily conscious lives most often happens over a period of time and can involve times of reflection and effort on our part to put into action the insights we have intuited. I have come to refer to these insights or declarations as moments of promise. Our task often is to decide how to act in new ways.

It is useful to acknowledge the contemporary issue concerning time in our culture, and to affirm a general difference between inner and outer times. We live in an era wherein we have a truncated sense of time as influenced by the media and the notion of "fast" – of many kinds including foods and deliveries. In the computer world, the quicker we "boot up," the better. Active imagination puts us in touch with energies from the depths of the psyche that stir up change in us; but this change is slow, almost imperceptible, and requires patience and courage. What is declared in the inner life, what is promised or anticipated, may take substantial time to manifest itself in any noticeable way on the outside. To have a life-changing insight is one thing, to integrate the insight into our daily living is another.

Years ago I had a deeply moving experience in active imagination that declared a change in me in the way I responded to negative feedback. At first I noticed nothing new and was a little disappointed. About six months after this dialogue, I had an encounter the likes of which for many years used to upset me deeply. I noticed after this encounter was over that I wasn't upset as usual and couldn't even talk myself into being upset once I became conscious of the fact that I wasn't. It was then I realised that the promise of the earlier active imagination experience was being integrated. Gradually, over time, my reaction patterns changed quite deeply.

Slow as it may be, we do change when we honour and seek to assimilate the experiences of active imagination. It is a transformative, healing practice. The healing that comes may have little to do at first with outside relationships or problems. What changes first and more deeply are our attitudes and opinions toward ourselves, the problems we entertain and life in general. Re-centring ourselves in that new mid-point stance between consciousness and the unconscious again influences this change.

The healing of our attitudes toward our lives is a fundamental benefit that we receive from the active imagination dialogues. It is quite possible that we will develop a broader sense of self, a more loving attitude toward ourselves, outgrow or move beyond our present problems, and revise our expectations of others.

Having stressed the importance of a change in attitude as a part of the healing process of active imagination, it is also important to affirm that some of life's issues are transformed and we can be changed in our fundamental character. The change of personality in this experience can run very deeply and be long lasting. So our healing may take either or both forms, changes in our attitude toward some of life's issues and deep level changes that result in our becoming a very different person. In my case the latter has come about for me through the active imagination experience that addressed my sensitivity to negative feedback. There has been for me deep healing in this regard. The former change of attitude has come about through an active imagination in which I came to relate differently to a back condition with which I have lived all of my life. This dialogue appears in chapter four. I remember a wise older woman once telling me that I would one day come to see my back as my best friend. It came years later and my attitude has changed from anger and resentment to one of acceptance and valuing my back as my close friend and ally. I still live with the condition, but with a very different attitude. Active imagination brings about a change in personality, one that is gradual, but pervasive; one that re-centres the person in a new sense of identity, one that can distinguish between what may change and what needs to be carried creatively, with dignity and even with purpose.

The *fourth* benefit that emerges through the practice of active imagination is a growing sense of personal authority in our lives. As we grow up in our various family, faith and cultural communities, most often we take on the values and opinions of those who raise us up. Our personalities develop in reference to these cultures. As we come into our adult years most of us will review and question those specific perspectives and values. I remember well changing my political party from the one held by my family as I reflected on a growing awareness of cultural and faith values that came to be important to me. Active imagination can assist us in developing our own individual values and perspectives for our lives. Conversations with members of the village can strengthen our confidence in how we see life and others and how we choose to live. We may find ourselves becoming more counter-cultural in terms of family, faith and social values. In a sense we learn to stand with firm conviction in our own place, supported by our truth from within. It will not ever be the "whole" truth for all, but it will be ours, and this authority can result in a deep sense of contentment in our daily living. The challenge will be to stand in this place with confidence and also with compassion and respect for others, and to maintain an expectant and listening attitude toward the ever new that emerges from our exchanges with the world around us. This is the eternal dance of the individual within the context of community.

The overall movement that has made sense to me is that we begin as referential people who move toward being self-referential. It was an observation by James Hillman, in his introductory forward to *Ecopsychology*, a collection of essays edited by Theodore Roszak, that challenged me to see a third movement. Hillman creates a third movement forward into being referential again, but now to the larger life of the entire creation. It is to recognise that we all live our highly individual lives in the context of human and planetary life and, in this third movement take our share of responsibility for the well being of each other and our planet. We move from referential to self-referential to "world-soul" referential. As our sense of personal authority is strengthened, we are able to choose how we will serve the common good, the larger life. Active imagination can assist us in making this third important step. One result of these dialogues in the depths of our souls is to realise just how bonded we are to all others and to a greater life soul. With this growing sense of personal authority comes a greater sense of responsibility to step up and act with intention for the common good.

The *fifth* benefit of doing active imagination is highlighted by a story about a rainmaker in China. He was asked to come to particular geographical area suffering from drought, and he broke the drought and brought rain by placing himself in harmony with the Tao. In reference to active imagination the relevant connection is that through our practice we put ourselves into right relationship with our own souls and with the essential nature of things. This may not change the flow of nature on a large scale, but it may well affect the flow of life with others and help us to live more responsibly with our larger natural environment.

The Rainmaker story is a challenging one to consider. Life on our planet in 2020 provokes us to consider more deeply what it means for us to be in right relationship with the essential nature of things. Climate issues are of extreme concern to any people paying attention to the health and well-being of our island home. Becoming "world-soul" referential has become of critical important. Active imagination begins with us making peace with ourselves. We seek to end our internal conflicts and also to risk giving shape and form to the internal dreams and aspirations that are hidden deep in the hearts of each of us. This will offer creative and healing energy to the common life that will put us, together, in right relationship with nature, with the essential nature of things, and with our island home.

As I have attempted to understand this for myself, I have come to an important realisation. The practice of active imagination over several decades has resulted in a growing sense of being at peace with myself, and being able to navigate whatever conflicts or tensions of diverse desires may emerge as live continues on. It feels like living rightly and honestly within, as if the civil war has ended. There will be small and large bumps in the road, but there may be no more dramatic surprises in terms of my reactions to life. It is radical inclusivity, every one who has emerged over the years has been welcomed into the village and contributed to the complex community that live within me. Further, I find that active imagination has given me a way to engage the unexpected in life, both misfortunes and blessings, with resilience, for purpose and with dignity.

In this section we have reviewed five benefits of active imagination practice. They are that active imagination: 1) enables a growing self-understanding, 2) diminishes gradually the dominant influence of the unconscious, 3) assists a change of personality, 4) encourages a growing sense of personal authority, and 5) opens us to a right relationship with the essential nature of things.

Some practical matters

Having reviewed these benefits we reflect now on several practical matters related to the experience. The *first* question that emerges from our experiences has to do with the frequency of these dialogues. How often should I engage in conversation with the people in my soul place, my village? As with most of these matters, individual experiences will vary. The most-practical measure is our present circumstance. There are times when we will choose to have a conversation with a figure from a dream that will be a one off experience. Therefore frequency isn't an issue. If an active imagination experience leads us to consider a series of encounters, then I have found that I need to leave time between the conversations to reflect on what insights are emerging and how these will influence my daily life. A few years ago I undertook a series of dialogues almost daily for several weeks with a child named "Solitude." The series was beneficial, but the intensity was almost counter-productive. Since then I have settled on the practice of no more than one conversation a week unless an unusual issue arises that invites more frequent encounters.

The issue here is to create time for reflection. It's not so much that we need to dissect the encounter, as to ponder what insights and potential changes seem to be emerging as we have these conversations, and what further conversations are desired. As I asserted earlier in this chapter, active imagination is an encounter in the symbolic, mythic realm of the soul, and it is best to accept the experiences as they are and not to apply detailed rational analysis to them at the outset. It is best to appreciate the experiences and their fruits as they are, so as not to inhibit the spontaneous flow of creative energy. I have had to learn to see myself as living a mythic story as well as a chronological, rational life. If a detailed analysis seems appropriate, it can come later when the initial numinous energy of the encounter begins to settle.

The *second* matter here is to affirm again the importance of having someone with whom to speak about our experiences. I remember reading that Jung had his clients only engage in active imagination when they were seeing him in Zurich. Active imagination, like many forms of meditation, involves a deliberate weakening of the control function of the ego. This is why individuals need a strong ego from the outset. The numinous quality of these experiences can be seductive and can draw us away from the ordinary tasks of daily life, and distract us from the sometimes-challenging tasks of integrating the insights into our daily lives. It is essential to have someone with whom to share, who honours the process. The functions of our companion will vary, but the overall task is to help us stay grounded in our present daily lives, and to consider how to use the insights of the conversations in ways that contribute to our transformation.

As part of this concern it is important to realise that it is almost impossible to connect deeply with another person's experience. These encounters are intensely personal and even after sharing with a companion we can have a sense of loneliness in that no one seems to "get it" as we do. I have found I need to keep my expectations in check and realise that I can set myself up for disappointment if I expect another to be as moved or dazzled by my conversations as I am. Likewise when I listen to peoples' experiences, I know I cannot crawl into then at the same level of depth and meaning as they do. It seems an obvious realisation, but it is important to be conscious and clear about it as we seek to share and receive counsel and feedback.

The *third* practical matter has to do with this sense of being grounded. When we are involved in active imagination, especially written dialogues in a series, we are well advised to ground ourselves in tactile, concrete, physical activities as a compensating balance. Such things might include gardening, sewing, painting a room, knitting, refinishing furniture, building something, or taking a walk or hike, engaging physical exercise or a sport regularly. The important thing is to get grounded in the everyday, ordinary activities of life. I remember well the woman who engaged in a series of dialogues who sewed up some new dresses and took up riding her bicycle each day. These more "hands on" sensate experiences help balance the compelling psychic energy of the active imagination experience.

The *fourth* matter here involves honouring the fact that active imagination is hard work. Engaged seriously, this work can be tiring both physically and psychically. Our encounters often take us into the unknown recesses of our psyches and we usually have no idea in advance as to what, or who, awaits us. We may find ourselves deeply humbled to review our present attitudes toward ourselves and others, challenged to make room for new aspects of ourselves that intimidate us, or invited to act from long held desires and dreams that free us to live more honestly and passionately from our souls. While our encounters in the long run may contribute to our self-understanding and a deeper sense of peace, we do risk paying a significant price for this. Every dialogue is an adventure that is to some degree unpredictable and can challenge how we are presently living in the world.

The *fifth* practical matter concerns our sense of reality. The intention here is to affirm that our soul work takes us into the realm of our personal, inner reality that is as important as our outer reality, the world of relationships, study, work, and our endless round of activities. Inner reality at times may seem *more* important than our outer reality, in that our interactions with our villagers often help us navigate more creatively and honestly our outer, everyday lives. It is important to remember that the reality of the inner life consists of symbolic images; it is our ongoing mythical story. Images in active imagination are real, the experience is real, but of an interior, symbolic reality. They are separate from our outer reality and we need to keep this boundary firmly in place when we consider the meaning and application of these vital, inner experiences.

In our present age this matter of reality is important for the recovery of the integrity of our souls, our inner work and our personal mythical stories that hold great truth. People who are beginning work with dreams and active imagination often have the tendency to dismiss these experiences as having no meaning or importance. It seems inconceivable at first that these stories and conversations, that somehow are independent of our conscious control, can have any meaning. In our time it is helpful to acknowledge our resistance to the mystery of the dream stories and the active imagination dialogues. With effort and openness to the adventure of this inner work, the integrity of these experiences can then become clear. When we are able to take the risk and make the effort to listen to the experiences at a deeper, symbolic level, we can come to understand them and apply their insights to our daily living. The challenge here is to be both rational and mythical people and to move with care between these two dimensions of reality, inner and outer.

In this chapter we have considered how to relate to what emerges in our experiences, again primarily in the written form of the encounters. We have considered some of the benefits of the experience and identified several practical matters. In the second part of this study we will look at experiences that others have shared as we seek a deeper understanding of the active imagination experience and its value.

Part Two

In this second part of our exploration of active imagination, we review examples that former clients and colleagues have given permission to use. As part of their involvement with this project, most participants have chosen their own pseudonyms, and the dialogues have been edited where necessary to insure anonymity. The participants are of various ages, and from different backgrounds; and most dialogues are encounters from several years ago.

To the reader, or listener, active imagination encounters may seem quite ordinary in content from outside the experience. Many years ago I shared a dialogue with a friend that was of great significance to me, only to have him comment in an off-handed way that he thought I had an interesting inner life. There was much more to it for me, and I learned to be more careful in sharing with others. For the individual in the experience, these dialogues are often deeply moving. Unexpected insights, startling challenges, and relieving affirmations all can emerge in the exchanges and leave us quite amazed at the wisdom that comes to us.

From my research work for my PhD years ago, I came to conclude that active imagination for most people is very much like a spiritual or religious experience. The dialogues are sacred in character. From my point of view, then, we enter here onto sacred ground. I thank those who have been willing to share their soul work with me, and now here with us, and trust that readers will catch something of the sacred nature and significance of the experiences as we attend upon them.

I have provided a brief introduction to each of the dialogues and offered brief comments at the end that both summarise the dialogues and point to themes and movements in the experiences. I hope readers will sit with these dialogues and allow the energy in the various mythic and symbolic stories to generate useful meaning and insight. For me, such encounters of the imagination will enrich us more by sitting with them, rather than dissecting them in detail. As I have mentioned previously, a detailed analysis may risk flattening the symbols and draining them of their deeper meaning. These dialogues are grounded in heart knowing, as well as contributing to head knowledge. It seems best to appreciate them rather than to understand them in detail.

CHAPTER THREE

The People we are

*At the deepest level of the human heart, there is no
simple, singular self.
Deep within there is a gallery of different selves.*
John O'Donohue

I am, myself, three selves at least.
Mary Oliver

Leigh's Dialogues

We begin our review of experiences with the dialogues of
Leigh, whose email I have quoted at the beginning of the
Introduction. The dialogues here took place almost thirty years
ago, and yet still carried a numinous quality when she read them
again during the 2020 Coronavirus period of isolation. Leigh
gives a brief picture of her life growing up: "I am an only child,
born and raised on the wide open [Midwest USA] prairie. In fact,
the motif that has endured is this: one small girl, small family,
small house, small town set by itself on the prairie." Leigh was
in her mid 50s when we worked together and she engaged in
these dialogues. She was married with three grown children and

in a job that was both challenging and stressful. She was also intending to leave that job, and she and her husband were planning to relocate to another town. For her, "Anxiety and the need/desire for control were ongoing issues." She also was dealing with a sense of resentment from expectations, both inner and outer, that asked more of her than she often felt she had to give.

In this first dialogue Leigh is anticipating the arrival of relatives for an extended visit. She is anxious and has tried to convince herself that they will have fun, but she is dreading the visit and no amount of reason seems to help. "Since I haven't been successful in getting a handle on it, I invite Anxiety into dialogue."

ME: Anxiety, what's this all about? M and J are easy people, quiet, unpretentious, not demanding. Is it just the time commitment, is that it?

ANX: More than that I think. I see you taking on way too much responsibility for the whole deal.

ME: Nothing new there. My head knows that I need not do that, but —

ANX: But what? Old habits die hard?

ME: I guess. But you know it's more. It's my old friend Control. It's a terrible stretch to be in control for that long and a terrible fear to think that I can't be.

ANX: So to just let it go, trust that it will flow along, not to feel the burden, What would that entail?

ME: It should be a great relief. To let go of the need to make all decisions, all plans. I mean – what's the big deal?

ANX: OK, what _is_ the Big Deal? They are coming here – your turf – and you've had others come. When you go to [another city], that's neutral territory.

ME: True enough. I just think this calls on me to give more than

I'm accustomed to giving. Time – energy – privacy – I feel that I am being invaded – that's it.

ANX: Wow! Powerful! Invaded, defenseless, vulnerable, at-the-mercy-of — all of that?

ME: Sounds pretty ridiculous, doesn't it? But I do just want to weep, to hide. I feel so much responsibility for [husband], some of which I need to let go of. This burden – and that's what it feels like – is way too big.

ANX: What if you incorporate your "live only today" approach?

ME: Might help. I <u>am</u> anticipating the whole two weeks. No wonder I feel overwhelmed. Deep breath, let it go, give thanks, enjoy.

ANX: There you go.

In the second dialogue Leigh describes herself as being "bent out of shape" and decides to engage with her Resentful Self. She is experiencing resentment as her husband plans to go to watch his brother participate in a seniors sporting event in another city. She wants some insight into why she is resentful.

ME: I'm <u>pissed,</u> as they say. I feel abandoned and left hanging. The reaction seems extreme to the circumstance. What's going on?

RS: Maybe it's the stuff you said last night. Resentment at [husband]'s even <u>having</u> a family. Maybe this really brings into focus how alone you are.

ME: It seems to. I am always aware of it, but I just go along. Then something like this. Besides, his sister intimidates me so. I've tried to deal with her as the genuine person I know she is. But I'm really scared (strong word!) about her coming here. I resent her and I don't want her.

RS: So what about her and her visit do you resent?

ME: She'll be getting in my way. There isn't space for her. She'll criticize and judge. I will have to give her food, time, attention – that's all!

RS: Wow, you're really upset.

ME: Right. I want to focus, in my usual single-minded way on the {city} trip with the diversion of [husband]'s party and the kids being here. That's all I feel I can handle, but no, this is foisted off on me without my   inviting it.

RS: So what do you want?

ME: [Husband] to stay home – no, I'd feel too guilty. I think he really wants and deserves to go. But I feel like if he goes, I've lost my back up – things won't be perfect!

RS: That's it, huh? Well, you said what you don't want. But what do you want?

ME: To be able to manage it with grace, without dumping a load of guilt on [husband], without putting him in the no-win that he's often put in   and maybe, having clarified my feelings, I can do that. Thanks for your help.

RS: Any time.

In both of these dialogues Leigh seems to gain a more steady ground simply by allowing the other voices, Anxiety and Resentment, to speak honestly with her. Each offers insight that enlarges her self-understanding and encourages her to approach her circumstances with a more open and confident attitude. Leigh experiences emotional honesty through the dialogues and comes to a more able and open attitude because of this.

Sometime later Leigh enters into the following dialogue to explore her feelings regarding her younger daughter. She reflects: "I find today that I need to write about my younger daughter.

I believe, out of the conversation we had last week, that she is still/again smoking. It absolutely sets me off. I feel not only angry and frustrated, but betrayed – way beyond disappointed. Therefore, I invite this part of myself, in all the complexity of feelings (my Feeling Self) into dialogue."

ME: OK, let's try to get a handle on this. I recognize that my well-acknowledged need to control is part of this. But it's more, much more.

FS: You've really stepped back, worked hard at giving each of your children space. Worked at the need to respect them as individuals and as adults.

ME: I have indeed. And if I do say so myself, I think I have done rather well. But this is <u>so</u> hard. I want to shake her, want to slap her. I am appalled at how primitive and how utterly emotional this is.

FS: And you'd like to come at it with your head, is that it?

ME: Seems like that would help. If I could really get a handle on what the components of this are – where I'm coming from – surely that would help.

FS: And what about where she is coming from? How does that fit in?

ME: I have a really hard time getting to that point – don't even want to acknowledge that she <u>has</u> a perspective.

FS: So what is there about this that sets you off so? I mean, there are all the logical and "right" reasons you have laid out to her, apparently to no avail – health, money, the offensiveness and unattractiveness of it, current "political incorrectness" of it – but what else? What <u>are</u> the emotions behind the fury?

ME: How dare she? My pretty little girl, my baby, the one who is so sweet and so precious, the one that I ache for and grieve for and worry so about. How dare she do something that is so overtly ugly and disgusting? I'm embarrassed and ashamed. It feels like (I want to say "is") a personal affront. An "in your face" repudiation of all that I tried (certainly more by example than by words) to teach her. It feels <u>very</u> personal. Somehow I have failed.

FS: Wow – that's heavy. How come this one thing comes together to symbolize your failure? Why is this so powerful? If you've failed, there are certainly other examples we could come up with. And why is it all or nothing – failure or success?

ME: I don't know. Clearly when looked at logically, it's an over-reaction. But I love her so much, want so much for her, see her struggle to pull her life together. And now – now – as she begins to do that – to revert back into such juvenile, self-defeating behavior —

FS: It's hard to know how much of this is about her, how much about you.

ME: Yes it is. My hunch is it's a lot about me. My need for control. My need for her to be what I envision for her. (But isn't it interesting that I don't agonize much about her being almost 30 and not supporting herself, that I grieve little about the unlikelihood of her having a marriage/home/family. One would think, those would be the "biggies".)

FS: Indeed. So what are you saying that you need from her? For her to be your perfect little blue-eyed curly-haired blonde girl? Your <u>little girl</u>? And when she acts in this way, you can't accept it?

ME: I hope that's not it. I hope I'm a little more balanced than that. I just feel so sad. My need (get that – <u>my</u> need) to be proud of her is very strong. And that need seems to be based on very specific behavior(s).

FS: And that comes from where?

ME: Strong family message certainly. A combination of disgust at my dad's smoking and seeing how it ultimately affected him and my mother's strong voice and disapproval speaking through me. Yes, in some odd way, this is a betrayal of her, that somehow I am letting her down, that I have not only failed my daughter, but somehow I'm failing my mother.

FS: Would your mother expect you to be perfect?

ME: She never did, never would. But I want(ed) so much to please her. And out of this, I inflict guilt on my daughter. The guilt bounces back and forth from generation to generation. What can I do, how can I get out of this circle?

FS: Always you want to <u>do</u> – it's hard to step back, isn't it?

ME: Oh yes. To just "offer it up", to give it time and space, to trust, to love, to realize that all is process, on-going – that's so hard. I want to whack her, to get her attention, to make her understand (and of course agree), to have it <u>my</u> way, to shape her up, to have her be "her own person" but on my terms.

FS: Unconditional love ain't all it's cracked up to be.

ME: I keep laying on the conditions. In subtle and not-so-subtle always, I keep giving the message that <u>this</u> is acceptable, <u>this</u> is what I want for/from you and, therefore, that is the condition you must meet. Whether I can turn loose more easily when she becomes a full-fledged (i.e. dues-paying) adult, time will tell. It's oh-so-hard to have this adult child – hard for both of us.

Leigh engages the complexities of her control needs, of family culture, and more importantly, of parental love. Most parents I have met over the years would have little problem crawling into this dialogue and identifying with the anguish, struggle, anger, embarrassment and aching love in wanting what is best for a child. The dialogue goes deeply into the complex world of parental love and challenges Leigh to step back, to recognize the limits of her understanding, to watch in silence and to continue to love, but from a little distance.

Leigh realised in sending these dialogues along that she really could not remember any specific benefit from them. I would venture to say they were helpful. The inner work expands our capacity to engage our outer lives more creatively. Leigh shares this reflection by way of conclusion: "I can make a more general comment. Without exception, when I framed the situation authentically, I found that the dialogue simply wrote itself. That is, I became the scribe and simply noted the dialogue as it came into my mind. This continues to seem like an almost magical process!"

Nic's Dialogues

Nic is a young man in his 20s. He has experience in public life through various forms of media and inspirational speaking. He has been active in the Christian way throughout his young life, including leading worship and offering reflections in that context. Over time he found that the interpretation of the Christian way of his younger years no longer satisfied him, and so he began searching for a new way. Nic became interested in soul work, including dreams and active imagination, as a new path for his spiritual life. Early on in his search the following dream came along and he then undertook the following active imagination dialogues. Here is the dream.

> *I arrived at my childhood home late at night to find it somewhat falling apart (walls stripped back to their bare bones in parts, dust covering everything, very empty, very cold, very sad) and completely dark. This is a house I so regularly felt alone in at night, and often scared too, and it feels sad and scary to be back here. As I walked through the house and made my way to my parents' old bedroom, I discovered an old man lying awake in the bed with a small, very dim lamp lit up, and a deep sadness in his eyes. He was lying on his side, not saying anything, but just looking lost. It felt as though he had given up entirely, and had been here for a very long time.*

Nic then writes: "Upon waking up, it became very clear to me that this man was a symbol of my loneliness, my biggest emotional struggle throughout my life." A few days later he undertakes this active imagination encounter.

(I come across loneliness (L) in a falling apart house in the darkness. He is by himself, without energy, devoid of hope. I have made us both a cup of tea and sit down for a conversation.)

ME: Why are you here by yourself?

L: Everybody else has gone. It is easier this way.

ME: But you are all alone, you seem so sad.

L: I am. (Starts to cry).

ME: There are people you could go to. Churches, community groups, surely you have some sort of family?

L: None of them would really want me there. I think it's best if I stay here. I'm not letting anyone down.

ME: But this is no way to live. You are worthy of so much love. You deserve to be loved. You are loved.

L: No, I don't think so. Everybody who has come has left soon enough. They've seen the real me. Annoying. Selfish. Sad. And they have left.

ME: I am not going anywhere.

L: I don't have the energy to keep this house in shape anymore. It's falling apart around me. But I just lie in bed all day. I don't have the energy to do anything else.

ME: Come with me.

L: Where?

ME: To a place you will be loved as you deserve.

L: I don't believe such a life exists.

ME: Nor do I entirely. But it's worth a try.

L: Please don't leave me.

ME: I won't.

Nic has made contact with one who represents the loneliness that he acknowledges as a part of his life from early memory. He is the middle child of three and somehow felt a sense of being lost in the middle. In the dream the childhood home is a falling apart, indicating that his childhood perspective on life is no longer of use and seems beyond repair. It confirms his need to shift to a more adult perspective on himself and life. In the falling apart home of childhood he discovers the Lonely man who lives there and yet is not able to do anything about the falling apart house.

The Lonely man is sad to the point of tears, and seems depressed, left behind, and forgotten. Nic sees him as worthy of love and in an act of compassion he invites the man to come with him. One of the fundamental principles of soul work here is that we cannot jettison or discard parts of our lives without suffering the loss. Whoever has been in our village, whoever we have been in the past, remains with us even if she or he no longer takes an active role in shaping our unfolding lives. Radical inclusivity is a key characteristic of wholeness. Whoever this man is, Nic invites him to come along "to a place you will be loved as you deserve." Neither is sure what this means, and Nic pledges not to leave him as the journey unfolds. Sometime later Nic goes to visit the Lonely man again in this second dialogue. In his soul work Nic has adopted the image of the inner village and he describes the scene as he begins.

It is late at night in the village. The moon is reflecting off the lake. Loneliness is in the kitchen making a cup of tea for both of us, which he brings out and places on the table on his deck. The sound of curlews calling can be heard echoing across the field. He is wearing a dressing gown to keep warm, while I am in my usual clothes.

ME: How have you been?

L: Much better, I think.

ME: I'm sorry I haven't visited much.

L: I imagine you like to think everything is better now.

ME: It does feel better, doesn't it?

L: Perhaps. But I hear you've been telling people you think you could quite happily never marry.

ME: Yeah. That might not be entirely true.

L: Of course it's not true. And it doesn't need to be either. You don't need to talk yourself into feeling more okay than you are.

ME: I think it's a defence mechanism. I'm terrified that I won't find somebody – or the right person – and so I'm just acting like I'm okay with it.

L: Why don't you think you'll find that person?

ME: Any number of reasons.

L: Tell me. Please.

ME: I don't think I'm good looking enough. I don't think I'm carefree or fun enough. I don't think I'm entertaining enough. I don't think I'm good enough. I don't think there's really any scenario where I'd be anybody's first choice.

L: Do you really believe that?

ME: Maybe. But maybe it's more a fear that the person I deeply desire isn't actually out there. Maybe she doesn't exist.

L: Maybe.

ME: Do you think she does?

L: I think you're still looking for somebody to complete you. I think despite your growth, you still believe that life will only really be worthwhile when you've found that other.

ME: I think you're right.

L: You're projecting to the world this okay-ness with being single, this sense that you don't need others to fulfil you.

ME: And I have made progress in that area.

L: You have. But you don't need to pretend you're any further ahead than you are. It's okay to feel this way.

ME: What happens if I never get married?

L: You'll have more time to read, I guess.

ME: But really, what will happen? Will I live in an apartment by myself? Will I change friendship groups every few years and have no real constants in my life? Will I feel always on the outer like I sometimes do now?

L: Why do you think you need a partner for a meaningful life?

ME: Because life is so overwhelming and sometimes so scary
      and hard to comprehend and I just feel like it would be
      so much easier if I was able to end the day lying next to
      somebody who I knew was going through it with me.

L: This not enough-ness that you feel by yourself. That's a lie.

ME: What do you mean?

L: A partner may come along, and it may be great. But you
      will be no more then than you are now.

ME: I just want to hold and be held. I feel embarrassed saying it.

L: It's not embarrassing. It's deeply human.

ME: Men aren't meant to want or need it though. And I know
      I'm not usually caught up in the male stereotype.

L: But this one has snuck in, hasn't it.

ME: It has. When I was a child, I went to bed with my favourite
      teddy bear Big Teddy every night. Holding him as I went
      to sleep made me feel connected, calm, loving and loved.

L: What happened?

ME: I became too old for him. I got mocked a bit for still being
      into teddies in grade four. I became ashamed of myself
      and hid him in the wardrobe.

L: And since then?

ME: I guess I've been wanting somebody to take his place every
      night since. The nights feel empty when I'm alone some-
      times. I wish I had somebody to fall asleep with. I wish I
      had somebody to hold.

L: The tenderness you felt to Big Teddy. The tenderness you
      feel to your idea of the woman who you might one day
      also hold. You still don't feel it for yourself.

ME: No, I don't.

L: Next weekend, let's go for a walk. I want to talk a bit more
      about that.

ME: Okay.

L: Right now though, it's late. And the night always amplifies the emotions. You should sleep. We both should.

ME: Thanks for the conversation. I'm so glad we are able to talk now.

L: So am I. These are conversations I've been wanting to have for years.

ME: Are you happier?

L: I am, actually. Not happy, but happier. Like you, it's a work in progress, and that's okay.

ME: I'll see you next weekend.

L: I'm looking forward to it already. Feel free to stop in any other time beforehand if you need to.

Things have changed. The lonely and sad man has taken on a new role. In the village he is living in a lovely setting in a home near a lake, and making cups of tea for them to share out on the deck. He now takes the role of questioning Nic in a way that is supportive and encouraging. It is not unusual for the person discovered in the abandoned or falling apart past of our lives to become a trusted companion and counselor to consciousness. Often such a visitor only needs our attention, our acknowledgement and the respect of our consciousness, to begin to change from someone forgotten, discarded, frightening, or perhaps never before known, into a trusted companion and friend.

In this second dialogue, the Lonely man becomes the friend and companion, who encourages through questions. He is an advocate for Nic and encourages him to realise that he is "enough" just as he is. He invites Nic to feel toward himself the tenderness he felt in his childhood for Big Teddy, and the tenderness he imagines as an adult he will feel for the woman he hopes to find and marry. The promise of these encounters is that Nic is growing into a deeper self-awareness and a greater self-acceptance. Having been welcomed in, the Lonely man is changing into a voice of deep wisdom and will be a trusted advisor as life unfolds. Their conversation on the deck in the quiet of the moonlight is a fascinating compensation for the loneliness discovered in the first encounter. Here loneliness seems transformed into solitude, lovely times alone in deep reflection. Often when we discover a painful quality in our lives, and engage it with compassion, this action allows its opposite energy to be released and expressed. Rather than being haunted by the loneliness of early years, Nic is now encouraged to embrace himself in solitude, with compassion. He is invited first to understand how to stand alone in his own life, to be "enough" as he is, so that he may enter into life-giving relationships with others.

Ann's Dialogue

At the time of this dialogue Ann was in her 50s, married, with three teen and adult children. She had left her involvement with a conservative religious organisation as was teaching middle school children in a government school. It was a role she found challenging. Ann grew up with a father who was alcoholic (now sober) and an unhappy mother who was frequently critical of Ann. This had resulted in Ann living with issues of low self-esteem and a deep distrust of women who tended to micromanage in their leadership roles.

In her place of work Ann faced a challenging task that involved meeting the needs of a woman that she had found a bit "pesky" in the past. She would have been happy to avoid the task, but she reflected: "I wondered why this was occurring now and felt there is something for me to learn, there is some meaning in the arrival of this event." She completed the task for the woman and this dialogue with the Inner Witch came soon after.

The witch figure had appeared previously in active imaginations; she was very challenging and appeared dissatisfied with Ann. Ann commented that she seemed at one time like a creator/destroyer image, and in another encounter was very critical. Her challenge was basically "you don't know who you are." In this encounter Ann notes: "she usually has a black pointy hat and typical black clothing and a broom, with a big nose." While it is not explicit, there is a change in the Inner Witch implied here through the change in her appearance.

Ann's style of recording her dialogues into her computer is to use the lower case for her own voice and the upper case for the other voice. I have left these lower and upper case distinctions as they are in the reformatting of the document. The two characters here are Ann – A; and the Inner Witch – W.

A: Dear Witch I am wondering if we are able to talk now, apologies about the delay.

W.   THAT'S OK DEARY.

A.   It's been a long time since I've seen you.

W.   YES IT HAS AT THAT.

A.   I am not sure what to say.

W.   MAKE UP YOUR MIND DEAR.

A.   You seem to have changed.

W.   YES IT SEEMS SO.

A.   You seem to be a bit of both old and new (she seemed to flicker between images)

W.   YES IT DOES SEEMS SO DOESN'T IT.

A.   You're not making this easy for me.

W.   SHOULD I?

A.   No I guess not. What is it that you want?

W.   JUST TO SAY THAT YOU HAVE CHANGED DEAR. YOU HAVE GROWN UP AND THAT IS GOOD TO SEE. IT IS NOT WITHOUT A COST THOUGH – YOU HAD A LOT TO GO THROUGH – AND YET THERE IS MORE AND IT WILL CONTINUE.

A.   I am wondering about the dream of the cottage – the woman said something about someone having taken possession of her mother's things so easily.

W.   DO YOU THINK SHE COULD HAVE BEEN TALKING ABOUT YOU DEAR? DO YOU WONDER WHO HER MOTHER IS? DO YOU THINK YOU COULD HAVE TAKEN POSSESSION OF YOUR HOME – FREE OF MOTHER? THE THINGS THAT WERE ONCE HERS BELONG TO YOU ALONE. YOUR SELF CARE, YOUR ABILITY TO DECIDE – ALL YOURS – DON'T YOU THINK? THE ABILITY TO WATCH AND BRING ABOUT INNER HEALING ARE ALL YOURS, FROM WITHIN YOUR OWN RESOURCES, YOUR OWN COTTAGE NOW.

A.   I feel very teary now.

W.   IT HAS BEEN VERY HARD BUT VERY WORTH IT, WOULDN'T YOU SAY?

A.   Yes.

W.   FROM THE TWISTED MAGGOTY WOMAN WHO DID NOT KNOW HERSELF, TO THE ONE WHO KNOWS HERSELF BETTER – YOU POSSESS YOUR OWN HOUSE. KEEP WATCH AND LEARN.

A.   Thank you, I suspect you have been keeping watch over me.

W.   INTERESTED ON THE SIDE LINES. INTER-FERING WHEN NECESSARY TO GIVE YOU THE JOLT YOU NEED.

A.   Is there anything else you wish to say to me?

W.   NO, KEEP GOING.

A.   I hope to talk more with you.

W.   AS YOU NEED. YOU ARE TIRED, YOU NEED TO GO.

A.   Bye Witch. I am not comfortable with calling you Witch. But it will do.

W.   YES IT WILL DO.

The encouragement from the Inner Witch invites Ann to continue to grow into a wider sense of herself as a self-possessed woman. She is challenged to take possession of her own house, that is, to claim her identity and soul. She is encouraged to realise that she can be free of the mother voices and influences, the outer mother still present in her life, and the inner mother voice that she took on from that family relationship. She is encouraged now to move beyond the influence of these old inner and outer voices and into a new sense of self-possession. The challenge is to continue to become the primary authority in her life.

The dialogue comes after the experience with the woman in her workplace because her attitude in that situation reveals to her the changes that have begun to take place. Months earlier Ann would have been quite distressed emotionally by this pending task. Over many years her encounters with demanding women and her own mother, as well as the internalised mother voice, have often caused her to feel like a girl in trouble again. In this instance she is only mildly upset and works through the experience with relative ease. She is growing into the woman of personal authority to which the Inner Witch refers. Her life is "all yours." She is taking possession of her soul house and becoming the authority in her own life.

Ann employs active imagination regularly with significant inner characters. The witch had appeared several times and had changed over time. Her appearance in this dialogue is a signal of this change. The Inner Witch has revealed more and more that she is an advocate for change and healing. Ann's final comment was that she actually likes this witch. She tells it like it is, speaks straight and yet calls her "dear."

Dean's Dialogues

At the time of these dialogues Dean is in his late 40s. His work is in administration for a large corporation. In his early years his family was involved in a conservative Christian tradition. While he was comfortable with this in some ways, it did not provide him with a safe environment in which to acknowledge that he is gay. He held this as a secret for many years. As part of his soul work he chose to write carefully crafted letters to his parents and siblings and invite them into an awareness of his sexual orientation. The family members received these letters with acceptance and this was very liberating for Dean. In this course of his inner work, he became aware of a critical voice that he named as self-loathing. This led to dialogues with self-loathing, one of which is the first here.

Dean: Hi Self-Loathing.
S-L: Hey

Dean: How are you feeling?

S-L: Tired. Sick of all this. My disgust for you has mellowed into a sort of resigned hopelessness. There's just no chance of anything going well. It's reached the stage where I don't even know why any more. You must just give off a stink of uselessness, the pheremonal equivalent of a big neon sign on your forehead that says "Avoid".

Dean: Why do you think I do that?

S-L: You're too desperate? You're not hot enough? Other men are too shallow? Bad karma? Who knows? Your singular lack of success is mystifying. Any witless, stupid, shallow, obnoxious dickhead in this city can get a girlfriend or boyfriend, but you can't, no matter how hard you try, no matter how many dates you go on. I mean, even I don't think you're THAT bad. And yet here we are.

Dean: So other men loathe me more than my own sense of self-loathing?

S-L: Yeah. Hooray. I win the self-loathing olympics. Oscar Pistorius eat   your heart out.

Dean: Do you feel loved?

S-L: Of course not. I do feel a little bit understood and respected. No one likes to think that they're just wailing into the night with no one comprehending what they're going on about.

Dean: Do you understand why I need to control you?

S-L: Hey, it's lonely at the top. I'd love it if you found someone who swept you off your feet. It'd be nice to be proven wrong. But I never am, because hey, here we are, 65 men dated, zero boyfriends. The pure objectivity of market forces is clear: your market value is zero. You are, literally and objectively, worthless.

Dean: Well in love, at least.

S-L: What other metric is there? You're nobody until somebody loves you. And besides, you're worthless in other areas too. You're lazy, clumsy, self-centred (but without the self-confidence that would make that acceptable), incredibly boring, pointless, unskilled, fat, weird and generally horrible.

Dean: I am not horrible!

S-L: You don't get too many opportunities to be horrible, but you would if you were competent enough to get away with it.

In the dialogue Dean is beginning to stand up to the part of him who represents his self-loathing. This voice has formed his opinions over years from his family, faith and cultural traditions. There has been much in these traditions that has been life giving, but Dean has also received clearly messages that have resulted in the development of the Self-Loathing voice. He has been with Dean for a long time. Dean continued to talk with him and stand up to him, and in this process he began to be aware of another voice within him who emerged some three years later. It is the "Ideal Dean" with whom he speaks in this second dialogue.

Dean: Hi Ideal Dean, how are you?

I-D: Stoic in the face of adversity. You?

Dean: Tired and pained and stressed and morose.

I-D: All four at once? Impressive.

Dean: Ooh, and lonely. And tired.

I-D: You already did tired.

Dean: Anyway, life feels in a bit of a hiatus at the moment. I've got mysterious back problems that prevent me going to the gym, and I'm on a post-holiday diet that prevents me from going out. And of course there's the parlous work situation, which I think is causing the back problems. Which is strange, because I don't feel overwhelmingly stressed, but my body is behaving as if I am.

I-D: It would be weird if we are so out of touch with our own emotional state that our body reacts long before it manifests in our conscious mind.

Dean: Weird and not terribly helpful.

I-D: There isn't really an ideal way to approach a situation that's completely out of your control. You wait until a challenge presents itself and you rise to meet it. You look for opportunities to hone useful skills. You focus on things that aren't completely out of your control and deal with those. You reflect on the people who are living rich lives whose challenges are far greater than yours.

Dean: I suspect that I also need to spin a positive attitude.

I-D: Adaptability is a great trait to have. You think that the direction our employers are taking is shallow and repugnant, but you also know that such a viewpoint won't hurt anyone but you. I know you can rise above it, while there will be plenty around you who can't.

Dean: On the personal front ... ugh, it's just depressing.

I-D: You still have many friends who enjoy your company, even if there's no one who cares especially for you. You should relish those friends. Find some opportunities to show that you relish them. You're allowed to be passionate and demonstrative – it won't make people hate you. Well ... not worthwhile people anyway.

Passion is deep. Cynicism is shallow. You're aware of this and you know how toxic cynicism is when it isn't kept on the surface, used as a seasoning rather than the meat. You're on the right track in being the instigator of more social activities, such as trips to the theatre. Less talk, more action! It will do you good.

Dean continued his conversations with Ideal Dean. They agreed to a regular time weekly to meet so that the conversations had priority and did not get overlooked in a busy schedule. They also agreed to a simple list of tasks each week that were positive in nature and affirming of Dean. During this time Self-Loathing was still around in the village, but he had gone quiet. Dean continued his involvement with his religious community, and affirmed himself by having a talk about his sexuality with the leader. This was a self-affirming action that also increased his sense of safety in the congregation. Over time his self-acceptance was strengthened by his soul work and he continued to feel more self-aware and as the authority in his own life. A sense of being settled in himself was growing in him.

Helen's Dialogue

At the time of this dialogue, Helen was in her mid 50s. Her professional work was in the field of mental health. The dialogue here is one of thirteen, most of which were in response to specific dreams. Helen did not indicate the dream context for this encounter. Helen undertook the dialogues "Because of the painful experiences I was having in my outer life." The series of dialogues covers a period of twenty months. The dialogue presented here is the sixth of the series. It is an encounter with one she names as the Hobo. There is no specific setting described for the conversation.

At the beginning the Hobo hands her a menu on the front of which is a tree with white birds in its branches. The text was handwritten and words here and there were illegible and Helen is not available for further clarification. Brackets indicate these places. The two people are: Helen: He, and the hobo: Ho.

He: What is this?

Ho: This is a menu I am handing you.

He: Why a menu? Am I hungry?

Ho: Yes.

He: How do you know?

Ho: Because I am part of you.

He: What part of me are you?

Ho: The part that has never seen the light – to date the part that needs to experience <u>you</u> – to help you to make You.

He: Why a menu?

Ho: Because I am offering you food – qualities of food – spiritual food but abundance of life and love also. Abundance of life is experiences – not always enjoyed at the time – but needed – needed for your growth – like the tree you see on the outside of the menu. You grow outwardly to correspond to your new experiences. You have already found that things you thought impossible a few years ago are actually very possible and that has come about from your taking things into yourself – [-] experiencing them coming to terms with them. You have surprised yourself and many others with the way you have coped with your situation.

He: I see the roots of the tree in good soil – but the roots also seem to be the shadow of the tree.

Ho: The shade is needed when things get too hot. If there were no shade we wouldn't enjoy the light, the sun. From where

88

you sit the shade envelops you – and it caresses you also as you have learnt.

He: What sort of food do I expect from a menu such as this?

Ho: We have a creative kitchen – we take pleasure from the simplest things. Learn to appreciate what is there. Never doubt that there is an abundance of wholesome food. Not only wholesome in the general sense, but wholesomely prepared for you – for your individual taste. If you learn to appreciate just what is available at all times you will never go short of life's treats.

He: What are the white birds?

Ho: They are the creatures of love, life and intuition. They are the very essence of the spirit of life. They come together to celebrate the feast which has been prepared before you. "In my father's house are many mansions …"

He: Is there more about the birds?

Ho: They are integrated with the life of the growing tree, they bring song – music and joy. They sew new seeds of thought and inspiration. [-] they are in couples – they work in harmony as couples, just as you shall do.

He: I'm working hard at being an individual at the moment.

Ho: Yes, but there is no reason why you should not be an individual member of a couple and you will. The birds will bring that peace – they may also bring the olive branch.

He: Why is the tree shaped like an hour glass?

Ho: In time your tree will grow large and spread right out and integrate many other things. At the moment it is contained – before long it will spread and grow and the birds with reproduce – it will blossom – yes, there will be an occasional dead limb and you will know how to deal with that. Soon more creatures of all sorts will enter and make their home and be clearly accepted – things which you never suspected would be likely to be welcomed – then your tree will spread and grow and stretch for the sky.

He: Is the blue behind the tree water or sky?

Ho: Both.

He: Does the MENU have other meanings?

Ho: The words are ME/NU <u>Me</u> and <u>You.</u> That is the two of us in harmony – the two of us integrated. The pure and the soiled – the light and the dark – The sky and the shade – When you have truly understood this, truly experienced it, you will know.

It also means MEN U. <u>Men</u> <u>You.</u> Your relationship with men will change – because you will become more related to the man in you.

He: Is there anything else you want to tell me about this menu?

Ho: You need to learn to be more experimental in your tastes. You may reject what you don't wish to have, but try – at least – Relax and try and savour everything that is offered you.

He: Thank you. Can you please explain about the newspaper cuttings? I can't remember anything about their content.

Ho: The contents don't matter. They are matter of fact, everyday, conscious content. We sometimes think they are truthful when they are not, because we tend to believe what we see in print. It appears to be logical. It is not always THE TRUTH. What is the truth for you?

He: The truth is something that I relate to as intuitively right. Something to which I can say "Yes – Right – I know!" I don't always believe what I read in newspapers.

Ho: Nevertheless the newspaper has facts. It is read by most people. It is written in a disciplined and studied way. The word discipline is one to look at carefully. It is there to tell you that it is all very well to enjoy the food offered by the menu, but the hard grind of discipline and order is always involved in the creation of anything. It must be grounded in the small print and the serious study – otherwise you may be seduced by the airy flight of the birds and not wish to enter into real life. For your full growth and spreading you must constantly check your truth – make sure you are living your truth and not somebody else's. And then to tell your story you must research and dig. Collate and then bring everything together with inspiration.

He: Is there anything else?

Ho: Newsprint is black and white. You must integrate both.

He: And read (red) all over?

Ho: Yes, and a little passion never went astray. Reading and research could be your downfall if you are not prepared to dig deeply enough for your facts before you create. [...] You are the instrument of process.

He: Lord, make me an instrument of your grace. Let me play fine music on my instrument. Let me stay well tuned to myself, to others individually as their needs arise. Help me to cope with my own needs well and allow others freedom to cope with theirs – and help if and when genuinely needed. Help me to know how to put myself in another's place but not to usurp others' right to experience. Help my instrument play in harmony with others staying well in tune.

In conversations with Helen we talked about her experiences with active imagination in this series of thirteen encounters. In reference to this dialogue with the Hobo, she remarked, "He was wonderful, I really enjoyed him." In two separate instances she remarked that she "moved to [her present part of the city] to find my hobo." It was his influence that helped her to realise that "it's okay to admit you're not perfect, it's okay … to let all that shadow stuff come up, and face it."

While Helen found it somewhat difficult to talk about her experiences, her reflections group around three essential qualities: change, learning and the sacred. Her sense of having changed was such that she looked upon herself in the dialogues and wondered, "Who is this poor little bugger? I don't know her anymore." At this she laughed. "Yes, that's me then, but I feel so different now, even in that short time." Her sense of change also affected her sense of physical presence with others, "even the way we meet people, even the way we stand, even the way we are with people … the way we move, walk, approach people … present ourselves." The core experience she had of learning was the sense of "great learning" that took her "deep inside, into yourself." She felt that she has opened up to a whole new and broader consciousness. The sacred character of these dialogues is summarised in a sense of "deep connection to the divine." She remarked: "There's a holy element to this, which I find extremely difficult to put into words."

In a final written reflection on active imagination Helen wrote "It is the only certain way that I have found to give me genuine and heartfelt answers to confusion and I find it totally reliable." She continues: "Both active imagination and what I described as religious experience are as real as my day to day life and have influenced and continue to influence this day to day life tremendously. I am in essence a very different person from the one I would have been had I never had these experiences."

Ed's Dialogues

Ed was in his mid 30s at the time of this dialogue. He had grown up in a conservative Christian community. It was a worldview that offered security and certainty for facing the world to those who were faithful believers. Ed knew from an early age he is gay and found it increasingly impossible to fit into the model that this faith tradition encouraged. He realised that certainty in life is fleeting at best and he struggled to deal with uncertainty, ambiguity and mystery. He had also suffered significant experiences of anxiety and depression as a result of the conflict between his sexuality and the points of view of the religion of his youth. For a time he participated in a faith based program designed to help men fit into a heterosexual lifestyle. Ed found it damaging to his sense of identity and the experience left him with significant anger. In addition to this, his father died when he was in his late 20's and he was deeply affected with grief in this loss. Another issue that he carried was a sense of feeling alone in his struggles. In the course of his active imagination experiences the image of the village square emerged as the place of meeting with his inner characters. There are two different experiences here that were connected as one.

Characters: Ed: Ed; Mi: The middle man of the three; End: The man on the end; V: A voice.

1. (Walking into the square of the village, there is a big water fountain in the middle. It has a lip on it where people can sit. There are benches around the square for people to sit on and there are many people around. There are some people sitting on benches, these are the established ones. They are well known to the ego and are trusted by it. I walk around the fountain and there sit 3 men on the other side. They are new to the square, like refugees recently been set free, enjoying the sunshine and freedom to just be and roam about. I go and sit on the side of the fountain beside them.)

Ed.   Hi. (They nod and acknowledge me.) I've not met you guys before. May I know who you are?"
      (I shake hands with them. They don't say anything.)
Ed.   Is there something I can do to help you to find a voice?
Mi.   (The middle one says) Yes. Listen to your body.
Ed.   How do I do that?
Mi.   Watch it, feel it, hold it, be in it.
Ed.   Ok. (I'm sitting across from them now, on a bench)
Ed.   Is there anything else you want to say to me?
Mi.   Relax, have fun, be kind, and good. Listen to yourself. Relax and you'll hear our voice.
Ed.   Are you in pain?
End   Yes. (Says the one on the end.)
Ed.   "What kind of pain?"
End   Heart pain, disconnected, apart, separated

(There is pressure on my view of the scene, like a thick wet heavy blanket pressing me down. Dad didn't do anything, I had to do it all myself. In [program for gay conversion] God didn't do anything, I had to do it all myself. Here with Active Imagination, it doesn't work and I have to do it all myself. The people don't speak to me, they never tell me who they are. They don't seem to help much, I have to do it all myself.)

2. (The scene is gone it's all black now, like a black hole, a vacuum that sucks even light into it. There is a pull towards it, I can resist the pull, but I decide not to, I move towards it and the pull grows.

I keep going and the force grows, soon I won't be able to stop it but I go on. Now I am moving through space without any anchor or hold. Just going further into the void.

I seem to "arrive" and I stop moving. I can now see millions of stars, little lights. But slowly the lights move toward me and it seems they are people walking out of the darkness towards me. There are millions of them. I can't see details of them just their form. They walk towards me. I'm just standing waiting, but feeling unafraid. They walk up to me from all around and they begin to reach me, they stop and place their hands on me, those behind them place their hands on their shoulders and so on till there is a mass of heads and arms all pointing inwards towards me.

I am connected to every living thing, not by accident, but by choice and intention. As far as I can see there are people connected to me by their own choice.

There is a sun, that begins to rise and I see that these people are dressed in all different colours, there is just an outrage of colour there is no pattern or design. The arms of the people then change from pointing inwards on shoulders, to embrace the people beside them, so that a million concentric circles are formed all around me. I ask who these people are.)

V.   They are the creation, all of creation.

(They begin to talk to one another and there is this mass of sound, much like the colours but a verbal version, all languages and sounds, but all speaking the same truth. They are speaking love. They embody love. The sun is setting now and it's going dark. The people are now gone but I don't feel alone, they reside with me somehow, and I am still connected to them. Somehow love connects me to them.)

In the first section of this experience, Ed is challenged by the three men to engage himself with more care and kindness. It is significant that the three appeared to be "like refugees recently been set free, enjoying the sunshine and freedom to just be and roam about." The three seem to represent an emerging energy of personal freedom and a positive attitude toward his body. He also hears the pain expressed by one and becomes aware of how alone he has felt. The three men now set free, say little, but they encourage him to begin connecting with himself, and this brings a deeper awareness of his feeling alone. The pain he feels is expressed by one of the three as "Heart pain, disconnected, apart, separated." This brief exchange is followed by a second experience that is a more narrative form of active imagination experience. Ed is drawn strongly into a cosmic movement that he chooses to let happen. He arrives in a cosmic space without any anchor or hold and goes further into the void. What at first appear as stars or lights become millions of people with whom he experiences a deep sense of connection. "They walk up to me from all around and they begin to reach me, they stop and place their hands on me, those behind them place their hands on their shoulders and so on till there is a mass of heads and arms all pointing inwards towards me. I am connected to every living thing, not by accident, but by choice and intention. As far as I can see there are people connected to me by their own choice."

The image of connection to all humanity in an amazing web-like structure stands in compensatory contrast to his sense of isolation from the first encounter with the three men. The web-like image is one of direct consolation to the pain of being alone, "disconnected, apart, separated." The Voice that speaks affirms that he is connected to all of creation. It is love that makes and sustains the connection. Ed is a deeply spiritual man, and the experience offers him a sacred image of connection to all of humanity, to all of creation. The imagery of the cosmos and the human web of connection are vastly different from the traditional imagery of his religious upbringing. Traditional Christian imagery would have been difficult for him to engage or trust. The experience of the cosmos and the web invite Ed to see himself as deeply connected in love to all of humanity and to hold his sense of being alone in this wider cosmic context of deep connection. One outcome from this encounter affirmed Ed's deep passion for work that supports the health of the planet. He continues to be deeply committed to environmental responsibility and renewable energies in his professional work ... and to "all of creation."

Jean's Dialogues

Jean describes herself briefly below. She was dealing with issues of boundaries, and issues of money, work and the creative use of her talents, especially singing.

The characters are:

Jean: a woman in her mid 40s, married, one child, vocal musician, voice teacher, and a health professional.

Rosa: an "earth mother," older woman, who is a nurturer but also an "eat, drink and be merry" person.

Shell: a younger woman who is very shy and will withdraw easily, but holds firm opinions if asked about things. She is very aware of how powerless people are ignored.

Sand: a "critical voice," doesn't seem to have a gender at this stage, but has a sardonic wit.

Big Guy: a tattooed, bikie kind of character, a gentle giant who is ugly and brutish but has a huge heart and a simple philosophy of speaking plainly.

1.

The two characters with Jean are Rosa and Shell.

Jean: I've been thinking a lot about borders and how my family of origin trampled through them all the time. It has been hard for me to have good boundaries of my own, or even to see the need for them – or that the lack of clear borders has made it very hard for me to get organised and to do the important stuff, the creative stuff; or even more, to feel "happy with my lot." Boundaries around friendship, family, work time, volunteer time – even clearly around myself, my physical space, my body, my own room. Not having a room of one's own … I'm wondering what insight you all might have about what is behind my fear of setting boundaries or the difficulty of keeping them.

Rosa: You're sitting here remembering lots of pain and time being alone as a child, being left alone or even abandoned by friends who didn't want to play, being isolated and thinking of reasons why you weren't any good – mostly coming down to being an "ugly" person – selfish, arrogant, insensitive. That's what you were accused of, and of course physical faults as well. You had a desperate need to belong, to have friends, and that made you accept all kinds of crossings of boundaries … Somewhere was a family full of love, life, joy, that if only you could find them, be accepted, be part, you would be living a real life. What you didn't have was a sense that you were ok as you were, and that other people would come to you as well. So you tried too hard and didn't respect your inner self – or listen to your inner self – enough.

Shell: You always wanted your own room or space, but then of course you have to occupy it, and be prepared to say 'go away' if you need to. I don't think you ever said 'go away' because people would, then you would be alone. Do you remember how afraid you were of being alone? How it is still one of your darkest fears?

Jean: You are both very right and clear here. What I am also remembering was the violation of my secrets that occurred when I shared them with my sister.

Shell: But you shared them because you didn't have the deep security to keep them to yourself. And you kept giving away things that you should have kept for yourself.

Jean: You are right – sharing secrets always seemed to me the "test" of whether you were friends of not. Imagining a friend as someone who knew everything about you and never betrayed you.

Rosa: The only person who is that friend is you, my dear.

Jean: So I betrayed myself.

Shell: Yes, I think so.

Jean: Somehow I have been blaming others for this leaking of my integrity?

Rosa: Well you weren't given a strong enough sense of your own wholeness and your right to yourself, and as a child you can't see that. But here and now you can. You can claim your inner sanctuary and you can make it real in your life.

You have to know how important it is, or you will spread out thinner than mist through the multiple demands on you – and one day you will disappear.

Shell: And the fear of disappearing is as bad as the fear of being alone – worse maybe.

Jean: Thank you both for this real insight.

2.

In this dialogue, two new characters appear: Sand and Big Guy.

Jean: I often have a deep sense of unease, a feeling that I can't "be" in my life- that to 'let go' will cause me to behave badly and suffer criticism. It wakes me up in the night, and causes me to behave guiltily; I feel I can't take time for myself, truly that my life is not my own. Whose life is it?

[Sand] Critical Voice: You would rather suffer all this guilt and remorse than take responsibility for your own life.

Jean: I would like to listen to what you have to say as I know your voice well, but not your name.

[Sand] Voice: You can call me Sand.

Jean: Because you get under my skin and irritate me all the time?

Sand: And because I'm always there no matter how much you sweep.

Jean: Come forward with your criticism.

Sand: There is a laziness in you, a sense that the world owes you a living, that money is just for fun and petty things and not for real stuff like bills and tax. You can pretend you don't have to be responsible, Daddy will bail you out, there's always another way to afford things. This puts you into conflict with (partner) because he doesn't have this delusion, or anyone to bail him out.

Jean: Is this why I don't take my work seriously, do you think?

Sand: It does seem like a hobby, doesn't it? You are hundreds of dollars behind every month, but what do you plan to do? Where is the concern for your situation?

Jean: I am very concerned – it is one of the things that wakes me up in the night.

Sand: But where is your plan? So much vague hope that things will improve – that is not a plan. Too much of your life has gone by with you just living day to day with no plan.

Jean: So this is an area I'm avoiding, all this stuff about money and being organised?

Sand: Yes! You can't handle money discussions, you don't want to know about your debts or your lack of income, you pretend as soon as you have a few dollars in your pocket that you are flush!

Jean: I have spent a lot of time in the past year thinking about these things.

Sand: Well you need a means of facing it more clearly – what percentage of your income goes where each week?

Jean: It is awful to do when I know there isn't enough.

Sand: Well what is your plan?

Jean: I do get the point here, and I will think about these things more.

Rosa: You know, your whole family has very complex and confused attitudes towards money, and it might be good if you could see that a bit more clearly.

Jean: Thanks Rosa.

Rosa: I also think you've got lots of talents you haven't used or explored in relation to making your life more viable.

Sand: That's a very polite way of saying you've wasted your life so far.

Jean: I don't think that's true exactly, but I do agree with Rosa that I don't always use what I have to the fullest, or think clearly about how to proceed.

Shell: All you ever really wanted to do is sing, and you hardly do that now. If you sang more and believed in it, you might find things were better.

Sand: but your singing is always full of doubt and self-criticism.

Jean: That's a bit rich coming from you.

Sand: Well you can hear it in the sound. Not enough heart.

Jean: I wonder if I could get you to stop listening so critically to the sound.

Sand: If you are not critical, you end up singing rubbish.

Shell: That's not true – no-one likes to listen to someone who is always criticising themself.

Jean: So if I could sing with a little less criticism and a little more heart, would that help?

Shell: I think so.

Rosa: You know I am for heart. Sing because you love it, forget about being "good" at it.

Sand: I actually agree. I can see how the criticism makes it a problem. But it doesn't pay the bills!

Jean: Yes, you had to put that in, that's the kind of thing my dad would say. How do you know, anyway? Could we try my suggestion?

Sand: Yes OK. I'll keep a little quiet on this subject.

Big Guy: I just want to say that I want to hear you sing, that's all. I really think it could be good and nice to hear. So sing and shut up!

Jean: Thank you all.

Some years after these dialogue experiences, Jean wrote the following:

"Reading through these dialogues from many years ago now, it strikes me how much wisdom is contained in them. It seems that this process of inner dialogue is a powerful way to access what we already have inside of us, even if we don't "know" that it is there or even believe that we have any wisdom at all.

When introduced to this process, I engaged a model of the human being which suggested that we were multiple, complex and sometimes contradictory; and that the aim of the work of Active Imagination was to discover and embrace this multiplicity, not to make ourselves conform to a more singular idea. The image of an inner family was very moving for me, especially as my outer family of origin was so difficult and I knew I was yearning for a different kind of family experience.

As I have continued over the years to engage with my inner family, I have discovered riches inside myself, answers to difficult problems, support through hard times, joy, wisdom; I have found beings, both human and animal, who speak to me and often surprise me with their perceptions of their role in my life. Because of this I rarely feel alone even in dark times. I am also more aware of the multiplicity of others, by knowing what I contain behind my ordinary façade. I know I am capable of surprising others as much as I am surprised by them. Even now, new characters appear in my inner family with a diverse perspective to offer, and I am grateful for them as I get older and I face different challenges. If I start getting too stuffy and conservative, the young people of my inner family remind me of the need for play, and the animals help me to find joy in the natural world. They also help me in my ongoing relationships with teenagers in my outer world."

The people we are indeed. Over years I have encountered writers who have asserted that we contain "multitudes" in our inner lives, our souls. Our inner villages include a wide variety of complex persons, who sometimes stand in opposition to each other and to our conscious points of view. In this chapter seven people have shared their encounters with anxiety, resentment, loneliness, self loathing, the ideal self, three quiet men recently released from prison, the Voice, an unusual and friendly witch, an odd man companion, and various women in conversation. Their work heightens our awareness of just how complex we are, and how rich and varied are our points of view. We see how it is possible that we do contradict ourselves, or rather, parts of us do not always agree, and yet we can create an inner life in which villagers learn to live together in some larger sense of harmony and oneness. Once we have met these people in the inner village, the notion of being a simple, singular self, loses its attraction. Embracing our complexity and the "parts of me" that we are, offers us a more rich and interesting life. To attempt to take refuge in a simple and singular sense of ourselves may well constrict our souls.

In the midst of this remarkable complexity, we can see that our active imagination dialogues have the overall purpose of helping us make peace within. The voices may challenge us sharply, but they do so to nudge, or urge, us along to a more comprehensive, inclusive and generous self-understanding. For each of us those who emerge will do so in a timely fashion, and will be unique to our needs and issues. For many of us they may have similar or the same names, like mother, father, child, wise one, hopeful, lonely, needy, angry, but they will appear in ways that speak into our individual stories. These encounters give personal and intimate shape and content to these unfolding stories, our own soul myths. The intent, woven into the dynamic of our dialogues, is to make enemies friends. Our hope is to support a growing sense of being deeply at home with ourselves. All this increases our capacity to offer others a deeper compassion in our interactions. Living with a greater peace in my village enables me to extend this peace and hospitality to others. In the next chapter we continue our exploration of these healing dialogues.

CHAPTER FOUR

Look Who's Talking: Other Voices

My good people of Gubbio, the answer is very simple.
You must feed your wolf.

Francis of Assisi

Most people I know who have had domestic pets, dogs, cats, birds and others, will confess to having conversations with their beloved companions. Sometimes the "speaking" from the pet is a bark, meow, chirp or other expression; sometimes it is a body movement that speaks to us in the ongoing relationship. Cuddles from our doggie, or the purring of our cat, are "conversations" we love to engage. Whatever the form of communication, it is an important part of our lives and a great help to our mental health. It is amazing how deeply these animal friends nestle into our souls over years.

In addition, how many times have I, or we, heard the advice, "Listen to your body?" "I am tired," seems to be a common response to the lives we have created for ourselves in contemporary society. Various scientific research projects in recent times have asserted that we actually have "brains" in our heads, hearts, guts and skin. Our bodies speak to us continually asking for relief, a break, a meal, a rest, a nap, or some exercise and activity. Our bodies challenge us continually to be honest with ourselves and to practice thoughtful self-care. I admit that at times I heed this advice well, and at other times tend to push on until I am forced to pay attention to my needs and limits. Perhaps it is my increasing age that requires me to listen with more respect to the everyday "comments" of my body.

Given these ordinary, common experiences with our loved pets and our bodies, it is not too difficult to imagine having active imagination conversations with animals and our bodies. The animals may appear first in dreams, and our bodies may suffer limits or pains that invite us into reflection and possible conversation. It may seem strange at first to enter conversations in this model of communication, yet the same principles and practices apply here as with people. Through the creative energy of our attentive imaginations we are able to animate these visitors, lend them our voices, and hear what it is they come to offer us. As in our dialogues with people, the animals and parts of our bodies come with insights to help us move forward in a deeper understanding of ourselves.

In this chapter we will consider some dialogues with animals and with parts of our bodies. In this chapter I join others here in sharing some of my own dialogues, and extend my thanks, again, to those who have shared their experiences.

Effie's dream and Dialogues

At the time of these dialogues Effie was in her early 40s. She was deeply involved in her faith tradition and also deeply involved in social justice activities. She was also participating in a training program for spiritual directors. Effie had a significant dream and two days later began the dialogues. There are four dialogues presented here. The first two came in quick succession, and several months later the second two came in quick succession again. Following the dream is Eddie's own initial reflection.

> Dream: "I'm seated on the toilet, and I suddenly realise that there is an elephant outside the toilet door. I'm conscious that it is a pressing, huge force, possibly friendly, but it might do unintentional damage. I scream for help. No one comes. Somehow I get out and find that everyone is in a huge dining area, talking about social justice, and comfortably having breakfast. Very cross that they have ignored my cries for help, I tell them to wake up to themselves. "It makes me sick," I say!"

This is Effie's initial response to her dream: "The following active imagination work flowed out of this dream. Issues of imbalance in my life need to be addressed. The dream suggests that social justice activities nourish a part of me, but I neglect other, more pressing, instinctual needs and demands – self-justice? Issues of suppression, loneliness, and an inadequate self-image are crying out for attention. The dream also suggests the presence of a large supply of inner wisdom, but also forces of destruction and anger, which can be harnessed for good, but cannot be ignored without harm to me in some way. My spontaneous connections and associations with "elephant" are positive and friendly, but ..."

The abbreviations are: E: is Effie; Es: is elephant, her name is given later on; L: is Lord.

1

E.   Good morning, elephant. I'm remembering my dream – I'm sitting in the toilet. I hear you outside. I stand up and I feel you pushing against the door. Who are you?

Es.   I am the deepest part of you, the biggest part of you. Some call it 'the heart of a person' – holder of secrets, full of emotion, memories, intuitions, instinct. I'm the non-rational part of you, your driving force.

E.   But why are leaning against the toilet door?

Es.   Because that's where you are at the moment. I just want to get in touch.

E.   Well would you mind not pushing against the door? I know you are friendly, but your weight scares me.

Es.   I don't mean to scare you. It's just that I've been roaming around for so long, I'm tired too. Do you think you could find me a stronger building to lean against and to hold you?

E.   It would have to be pretty big.

Es.   What about a cathedral?

E.   Where would I find a cathedral?

Es.   You have the resources within you, but first you'll have to move out of the toilet.

E.   I'm glad to. There's no room, no one else there, no escape route. It's just an outlet for my very basic physical needs. Where I dump my waste. I feel wasted at the moment, waiting for something or someone to happen. My work is very lonely and I wonder where it's all leading.

Es.   You have deep instincts to love, to be very compassionate, to inspire; but you've been locked in. I want to help you to get out and build the cathedral – a place for the God within. I am your deepest Self. Your outer self needs more support quite urgently …

2.

E.   Good afternoon elephant. I'm wondering whether I understood who you really are. I'm seeking some clarification
about your identity. It's very important for me to know
who you really are.

Es.   I've told you. I'm your innermost and outermost Self, your
heart seat, instinctual feeling, intuition, largesse.

E.   Thank you for not leaning on the toilet door.

Es.   Why don't you open the door and come out and touch me?

E.   I'm frightened of getting too close to you. I might acciden-
tally get squashed.

Es.   You've got more chance of getting squashed in the toilet.
No escape there. At least you can jump out of the way if
my largesse threatens you.

E.   I'm sorry if I have hurt your feelings, but even elephants
have been known to turn nasty. I remember the story of a
famous elephant at a zoo. She was shot because she hurt a
child, I think.

Es.   That's possible, but I have no intention of harming you.

E.   Can you move away from the door about a room's distance,
please?

Es.   Okay. I see that you don't quite trust me, but I understand.

(I step out of the toilet and I see a big warm-faced Mother elephant
with a baby elephant almost hidden from view. They are playing
together. The mother squirts the baby with water. I think this is a
lovely sight; I move a bit closer, still a bit afraid.) Would you like
a ride on me?

E.   No thanks. I couldn't get on, or stay on, without a halter
or a hoist.

Es. Another time.

E.   Would you mind getting down and having a rest on the ground, so I can have a closer, eyeball to eyeball talk?

Es. That's why I suggested a ride, but anyway I'll do as you ask.

E.   Thank you very much.

Es. You have thought about the cathedral?

E.   Vaguely.

Es. Yes, that's how you'd think. Too much clarity limits dreaming anyway, so don't worry about the vagueness.

E.   What should I do to resolve the crisis situation?

Es. Who says it's a crisis situation?

E.   G.

Es. Well he ought to know. I guess it is.

E.   That's what I thought.

Es. Well I'm not quite sure yet. You went to see X. That's good. You stepped out. You know you're not living to your full potential. I'm bursting with ideas, and yet you remain so confined and insulated.

E.   Is it wrong to have the … (a country property)?

Es. Not at all. It's not the (property), or X or Y or Z that's stopping you. It's you. You don't believe in yourself, and so you have confined yourself to the smallest possible space.

E.   How can I believe in yourself/myself?

Es. Read scripture. Read other people. Believe in the truth.

E.   What about my sickness of social justice activities?

Es. They're okay, but you need other outlets.

E.   Like what?

Es. That's up to you. Keep your eyes open. Trust your intuition and get out a bit more …

3.

(By now I have given the elephant a name, Esther, and have completed a year in a training program for spiritual directors, where I have been encouraged to "believe in myself.")

E.   Lord, I am a bit weary today, but I'd like to have another chat with Esther. Please be with us.

Es. You are very tired, and that's all right. Your days are fruitful, though you don't think they are. Thousands of little activities, they all add up.

E.   Today I was thinking about losing the present ego – to let some of the unconscious come through. I've read somewhere in Scripture, "I am what I am by the grace of God, and this grace in me has <u>not</u> been fruitless."

Es. Yes, you can't claim anything of yourself. It's all gift. Your part is to acknowledge the gift and use it.

L.   I want you to live to the full. There is much to be shared. Don't be scared.

E.   Well Lord, I have a little, ever so tiny dream about the nonviolent life style. I guess we've tried to live it in our work … I wonder if I could do something, make a contribution in that area.

L.   My life was about nonviolence. The world has still not grasped the message. Why not give it a go?

Es. It will take elephant strength of spirit. You've been praying for years for direction. Nothing has been lost.

E.   I get so tired.

Es. That's because you don't believe you are doing anything worthwhile. Once you're enthused you'll be energised.

E.   Do you mean that what I have been doing has been a worthwhile contribution?

Es.   Of course it has. Nothing but good can come of it. So much prayer and goodwill. Believe in your gift – and let go with enthusiasm. You are not easily convinced you know.

E.   Well it's so easy to deceive yourself.

Es.   Well if you can't trust your own judgment, trust the judgment of those you respect.

E.   I guess I need to think more clearly about making the most of present possibilities. Why am I looking for some elusive something over the hill?

Es.   There's nothing wrong in looking for the 'more.' From where I stand I can see quite a distance, but I'm happy to be in the present also. By the way, how's the cathedral coming along?

E.   I'm not sure. I feel I need a bit of help in that direction. Wait a minute. Perhaps losing my limited ego is part of the reconstruction. Letting the gift out is part of the process. It's all God's work – making a larger place for God, by trusting in God's gift.

Es.   I think you've got it.

4.

(I've been doing some reflecting on the spirit d'evil as the 'put down spirit.' The Holy Spirit being the 'Spirit of Uplift.')

E.   It just occurred to me Esther that you could lift a person 'off the ground' into an 'uplifted position.' I wouldn't mind being lifted up. I really love that picture of you walking with your baby underneath – towards the tree of life. You look pretty old and worn though.

Es.   It's good to grow old and worn. That leads to the next stage.

E.   What about the little elephant?

Es.   That's you coming to birth again and again. We are always changing. New life has come to you. I will help you protect and nurture it.

E.   Thank you dear elephant. I guess you are wise enough now to do that as you have been going for centuries. I realise I can draw on your wisdom but not claim it as my own.

Es.   Oh, heavens, no. It's not your wisdom. It's part of a stream from ancestral times. You are somewhat negative about the bad stuff that got passed on. Rejoice in the good.

E.   Okay, I will.

Es.   I'm going to lift you up, but you'll need lots of trust.

Effie's receives a visitor outside the toilet door in the form of an Elephant. The quiet humour of this cannot be overlooked, as Effie is a small, slightly built woman. She also has in her manner an infectious, lilting laugh, into the spirit of which one is easily gathered. We learn in the dialogues that the elephant is a mother and with her is her young one. Whenever the newborn or young are present we get the sense that there is positive potential for the future in the encounter. The toilet may seem an odd place to begin these dialogues. Effie is getting rid of material no longer needed. It is waste material that will be injurious to her if she tries to keep it. It is a humble meeting place for an encounter. Effie is in a vulnerable place. These are signs of being open to, and ready for, change.

The elephant, that we later learn is Esther, identifies herself as "the deepest part of you, the biggest part of you. Some call it 'the heart of a person' – holder of secrets, full of emotion, memories, intuitions, and instinct. I'm the non-rational part of you, your driving force." Later Esther identifies herself again: "I'm

115

your innermost and outermost Self, your heart seat, instinctual feeling, intuition, largesse." Given Effie's life long immersion in her Christian faith tradition, it seems appropriate to see this unusual visitor as representing the sacred life, the divine energy. Here is the divine life, the deep wisdom of the soul, in a different, surprising and compensatory form, coming to call out forgotten or repressed aspects of Effie's life and soul. What can it mean that this sacred life takes the form on a mother elephant with her young one? What ever else Effie may make of it, it is an image that implies a deep instinctual maternal aspect of her life. It is also free of layers of interpretation from the spiritual tradition that has nourished her and also contributed to her wounding.

In her initial reflection, Effie names the issues she needs to address. She is caught up in self-injustice, while actively supporting causes of social injustice. She acknowledges that she experiences loneliness, and that her self-image is wounded. In the face of these issues, Esther the elephant comes to be an affirming presence for Effie. The suggestion of a cathedral makes sense in the context of Effie's Christian worldview. Esther suggests a large cathedral building on which she may lean, but that will also hold Effie. Her present spiritual container is far too small for what Esther has in mind. Later the Lord picks up the same theme and says: " I want you to live life to the full." The dialogues with Esther affirm that our present spaces for the soul, our attitudes and self-understanding, may no longer hold all that life intends for us.

Debe's Dialogues

The following material is from Debe, who was in his 50s at the time. He was married with grown children. His career work was in human services. These dialogues took place during a time of significant career transition for Debe. The initial narrative describing climbing the rock took place on its own. Sixteen days later the dialogues began and took place over another week in brief passages, amongst dreams and reflections. Following Debe's own markings of the journal pages, I have pieced together the three weeks of encounters as one dialogue so that they flow as one single story.

In the Dialogue are: Me: Debe; SV: Soft Voice –a small bird; LD: Little Dog; BB: Black Beetle, and SS Sandstorm.

(I feel so frustrated and angry at the difficult climbing situation on the rock, I hit the wall with my fist. Uselessly – worse. I lose my grip and fall to the ground to the soft sand. I lie there, the breath knocked out of me, hurting and tears rolling from my eyes. I can't call for help – I don't know how to overcome the problems – I sense the strength of the rock beside me and around me and become calm and just lie there …

(16 days later) I sit up, having regained some strength and feel thirsty. SV comes flying up the crevasse.)

SV: There you are! We have been worried about you.
Me: I slipped off the rock face, and I was too hurt to move, but I'm improving now. Do you know the way to some water? I'm thirsty – I guess the other two are too.
SV: They're ok – they found a little stream near the mouth of this crevasse, but stayed there waiting for you.
Me: Well let's not keep talking – let's go so I can have a drink.

(We walk along with SV on my shoulder)

117

Me: Where do we go from here, SV? I sense there is something beyond this rock, perhaps in the desert, perhaps beyond it. I started to follow you before – I'd like to continue now.

SV: You need to gain a bit more strength yet.

Me: I feel anxious as well as thirsty – I want to get on, get moving. It's frustrating just waiting about. Yet there are also dangers ahead, and I feel afraid too.

(We come around the corner, and there lying in the shade are BB and LD.)

Me: It's good to see you – where's the stream you found?

BB: LD found it down low here, behind this lump of rock.

Me: Not that I looked, but it is sure hard to see!

(I lean down and drink. The water is cool and beautiful. When I stand up again, and just catch a glimpse of SV as she flashes ahead, turning into the desert deeper.)

BB: She doesn't wait around.

Me: She suggested we wait though, till I'm a bit stronger. I think I need to, certainly overnight, and then we'll follow her lead.

BB: We've come this far, we might as well continue.

(We lie down under a little shelf of rock as the cool air begins to get colder, and huddle together for warmth and sleep. In the morning we set out in the direction that SV took. We walk freely, being well rested from our sleep, and travel a fair distance. It begins to get hot and oppressive, and the cool wind which had been blowing across us dwindles and stops.)

BB: Look over there! Those clouds don't look too good to me! I think we should turn back and seek protection at the rock.

Me: I agree that it looks like a storm brewing – but it's so hot! Perhaps it will be a sand storm – It's not good! You're right!

LD: I'm sure I caught a glimpse of a small oasis some way ahead. I reckon we press on as fast as we can.

Me: That's great! My two advisors suggesting directly opposite actions! What now!?

(BB leaps at LD)

BB: I'll just pick you up and carry you back to shelter!

(But LD is too quick and darts ahead to stay out of reach.)

Me: That's no good – force isn't the answer BB!

BB: Well what are you going to <u>do</u> then? What's your answer? The storm could kill us all!

Me: I don't <u>know</u>! Stop talking while I think …
There may not be much time, I just don't know, but LD your oasis looks almost too attractive! Are you sure that's where SV went? Can we talk about this for a bit?

LD: That's certainly the direction I last saw her go – she seemed to be going straight for it.

Me: Well, I remain uncertain – it looks good, but it may not be much protection if the storm really hits. And BB, I feel as if I've left the old country now – it's still there for me, but I don't find it appealing – not at the moment, anyway, even with the storm coming. In fact, we've come too far to even make a run for the rock. I guess you'll think I'm mad, but I believe the answer is <u>in</u> that storm.

BB: What do you mean?

Me: I think we set out towards those clouds.

BB: You are crazy! I could fly you back to the rock …

Me: What about you taking LD back there? I'd be happy to see you safe – go quickly! The wind is rising.

BB: Come on LD – let's go! Look after yourself Debe.

Me: You too! Bye!

(They fly away, and I turn to face the clouds of sand, whipped up by the wind and start to walk into it. The wind is hot, and the sand whirls around, but I am not touched. It gets darker, more violent, yet I can stand. I sense some great power, and feel amazed, but become confused as to my sense of direction, and decide all I can do is sit down in the middle of it all and wait …

(3 days later)

As I sit I hear music, and remember words from the distant past – Psalm 145, vs 5: "I will meditate on your glorious splendour; vs 20: "You preserve all those whom you love …)

Me: Sandstorm, you are powerful and marvellous in my eyes, you are nurturing me and holding me safe; you have the shape of God; will you speak to me?

(I sit expectantly with joy in the music of a Bach Partita on piano and the swirling darkness continues.)

SS: I am with you always.

Me: You are the Lord. How great to be here! I want to know which path to follow, yet I cannot see. And I worry about my responsibilities to my friends BB and LD, and the others back there behind the desert edge.

SS: Whatever you decide will be OK – I love them too and will care for them.

Me: But I don't want the pain of mistakes, either for myself or others.

SS: Can you stop the whirlwind?

Me: What do you mean?

SS: I surround you with darkness and a violent sandstorm. You cannot tell the centre from the edge, but you want to move. You cannot stop the whirling wind, but wherever you move I will be with you and you will be able to bear whatever happens.

Me: I don't know what to say. What you say is marvellous, strengthening and reassuring to me, and I want to give you thanks. But I feel my words are so small, like a prattling brook. I'll just sit here a bit longer, I think, and wait on you …

SS: Sit away, my friend!

While these dialogues took place over twenty years ago, Debe and I had opportunity to reflect on these experiences again. In our conversations Debe shared about the origins of his animal companions and the sandstorm that are central to his journey. He writes: "The bird could well be based on the parental family budgerigar we had when I was about 8 years old. It loved pottering around on the floor, and it very sadly met its sudden end when I was washing dishes and stepped backwards. The little dog was very much in the image of a favourite terrier that was well and truly alive at the time of these dialogues. Dust storms were not common, but often enough over the years where I lived, so would have added to my feelings being inside the sandstorm. At the time of the dream I remember strongly relating the whirlwind to the image in Job 38:1, and the sense at once of security and great hazard. As for the black beetle, I can't relate that image to other experiences beyond exploratory childhood life in general, growing up in a new suburb on the edge of bushland. It was a surprising image in the dream that led to these dialogues, and I seem to think it was at first a water beetle, certainly able to swim underwater carrying me within a bubble or air in one sequence that comes to mind."

After these dialogues were complete, Debe came to see something of the Christ in the Black Beetle. He noted that the size of Black Beetle was never clear. At times the beetle seemed of normal size and at times the beetle was large enough to carry Debe to safety. During these dialogues Debe purchased a black stone and silver ring that he wore as an act of honour for Black Beetle and the dialogues. It was his way to connect the inner process to his outer life.

There are also associations of divinity to the sandstorm. The sandstorm seems to be an intentional event. It is created by the voice of the sandstorm and Debe is placed in the midst of it. He stands in the midst of utter confusion and cannot find his direction, yet he is unharmed and assured that he is safe. He submits to the option to wait. This sandstorm event has the sense of an experience of ritual testing. The test seems to challenge Debe to trust this process in which he is involved. He must risk being in what could become a dangerous experience. In the midst of his confusion in the sandstorm, Debe has to trust the voice of the sandstorm assuring him that he is safe and that things will work out. At present he seems to have done all he can do.

This symbolic ritual testing related directly to his time of career transition. In his outer life Debe was in deep conflict and feeling very ambivalent about what direction to take. It was a deeply unsettling time and he had to trust that his efforts to create a new way forward would bring positive results. At this point all he could do was to wait. He noted that the resolution to his outer career transition came about two weeks after he completed these active imagination dialogues.

Ann's Dialogues

We encounter Ann here again. In chapter three she shared her dialogue with the witch. There are two active imagination encounters here that are just over two years apart in time. The central figure in the first is a tiger and in the second a lion with other insects and animals present, including tigers and lions. Both Tiger and Lion have been a part of her village for a while.

1.
A: is Ann; Ti: is Tiger; Men: the men with an elephant.

A: Oh tiger I have missed you so much. He stretches I pat his head. There are some indigenous people with him.
Ti: COME WITH MY FRIENDS.
A: Ok where are we going
Ti: YOU'LL SEE.

(We are walking through the jungle it seems. The men carry spears, and wear grass skirts and rings in their nose, long hair. Painted faces. Tiger is up front walking they are kind of dancing behind.)

A: Tiger can I go up front with you?

Ti: NO YOU MUST WAIT BEHIND.

(More men have joined us – with red turbans they are walking or riding an elephant. I am confused.)

Men: COME, YOU MUST KEEP UP.

A: All right, where are we going?

Men: YOU WILL SEE.

(We come over a hill and I see a sandy racetrack. I see tiger ahead. There are many different kinds of people, roman soldiers shooting arrows, even lining up for foot racing. There are many people, cheering competitors on. It seems to be a big event. I am totally confused.)

A: Tiger what is this about?

Ti: YOU DO NOT KNOW?

A: No, I do not know or understand. Please tell me.

Ti: THIS IS YOUR INNER WORLD, IT IS ACTIVE AND VIBRANT THERE ARE MANY MEN HERE – WHERE ARE THE WOMEN? YOU MUST FIND THEM AND RELATE TO THEM, FOR YOU ARE A WOMAN AND YOU MUST KNOW WHAT IT MEANS TO BE WOMAN.

A: Tiger I am upset now – I do not like being woman.

Ti: YES AND YOU MUST FIND OUT WHY BECAUSE THAT IS WHAT YOU ESSENTIALLY ARE – WOMAN.

A: How can I find more – I mean I have spoken to women in me.

Ti: YES BUT NOT ENOUGH. YOU MUST DELVE INTO THE EXPERIENCE OF YOURSELF BEING WOMAN.

A: You know I will not like that delving at all.

Ti: YES I KNOW THAT AND THAT IS WHY YOU MUST. HOW CAN YOU CAN BE FULLY WHO YOU ARE IF YOU DO NOT FIND YOUR WOMANESS?

A: Does it really matter?

Ti: YES IT DOES BECAUSE THAT IS WHO YOU ARE – WOMAN. AND YOUR EXPERIENCE OF BEING WOMAN IS WHAT YOU MUST FULLY ACKNOWLEDGE IN ORDER TO BE WOMAN FREE FROM THE PAST AND REACHING INTO THE FUTURE – UNFETTERED. YOU MUST DISCOVER WHAT IT ALL MEANS TO YOU, YOUR EXPERIENCE OF BEING WOMAN. AND WHAT YOU WILL DO ABOUT IT. THEN YOU WILL HAVE A VOICE, THEN YOU WILL HAVE THE COURAGE TO SPEAK, THEN YOU WILL NO LONGER BE FETTERED BY A TYRANT, WHO DOES HOLD YOU IN A WAY YOU DO NOT YET KNOW. YOU MUST BE FREE OF HIM. YOU WILL MEET HIM AND YOU MUST BE READY. THE WITCH CAN HELP YOU, SHE IS INQUISITIVE. PERHAPS YOU NEED TO GET TO KNOW HER MORE, UNDERSTAND HER AND WAIT FOR HER HELP.

A: Are you going to take me to the women I must meet?

Ti: ONLY IF I HAVE TO – IF THEY ARE DEEPER THAN THEY NEED TO BE. AND SOME MAY BE OUT OF REACH FOR THE MOMENT. BUT OTHERS WILL

COME. YOU HAVE MET SOME BUT THERE ARE MORE. YOU ARE IN A MAN'S WORLD – IT IS TIME TO COME OUT OF IT.

A: Can I ask about the lava men?

Ti: YES SURE.

A: How do I learn to surf the lava flow?

Ti: THEY WILL TEACH YOU THAT. BUT FIRST YOU MUST FIND MORE WOMEN AND KNOW THAT THE ENERGY SOURCE IS ALWAYS FLOWING, IMAGINE IT AND YOU WILL HAVE A SENSE OF IT. LET IT FLOW THROUGH YOU, THIS IS NOT YOUR ENERGY BUT IT FLOWS THROUGH ALL THINGS, OPEN YOURSELF TO IT AND BECOME WHO YOU ARE.

A: So do I look for you?

Ti: YES YOU CAN LOOK FOR ME – I WILL BE HERE.

A: Can you take me to where I need to go – I am quite fond of you, you reassure me when you are present.

Ti: OK I WILL TAKE YOU. TAKE A LOOK OVER THE FIELD – THEY PLAY ALL SORTS OF GAMES – THEY HAVE PLAYED WITH YOU. IT IS TIME TO FIGHT BACK AND REGAIN YOUR WOMANESS. SHE OF THE EARTH CALLS YOU TO FIND YOURSELF AS WOMAN, YOUR ESSENTIAL NATURE. SHE HAS WHISPERED TO YOU BEFORE – LET HER WHISPER AGAIN. YOU MUST LEAVE NOW IT IS TIME FOR YOU TO GO.

A: Yes I think I am getting distracted now.

Tiger, her companion, takes her to see the activities of men. The men here are from other, different cultures, and from ancient times. Tiger asserts that this world may be familiar but now represents "a tyrant, who does hold you in a way you do not yet know." Her challenge is to move out from the world of men, the masculine, and to search more deeply for the world of women, the feminine, and her own sense of being woman. Ann tells Tiger that she does not like being woman and is hesitant in the face of the task, but Tiger insists it is her challenge to regain her identity as woman. The focus of the search seems to be for a sense of being woman that is more connected to the earth. "She of the earth calls you to find yourself as woman, your essential nature." He suggests that the witch can be a helpful companion and guide.

2. A: is Ann; V: a voice; Li: is lion; WW: is wild woman.
(I close my eyes. At some point Tiger appeared from behind a curtain/screen on a stage. Lion also walks out and onto the floor. He is standing in the light from an open doorway and walks towards the door. I follow. It is hard to follow, I start to float above, looking down on Lion.)

A: Put me on the ground.

(After a bit of difficulty … I eventually find myself with Lion at the edge of a waterfall. Lion jumps across to a dark ledge and I follow. I am in a cave like room. A strange small man is walking around (goblin/elf like?) I find it hard to move, I am too big for this room.

V: You have to learn to crawl.

(I get on my hands and knees and try to crawl. I see a praying mantis outside the room, so I figure I must be smaller. It is difficult but I manage to get out of the cavern. I see ants and crawl with difficulty to follow them through soil. I end up in the egg section.)

V: They are moved to grow.

(A strange looking ant comes into the room and picks up an egg, I follow. I am heading upwards in what must be the ants' nest. There are some antlike creatures pulling a dead insect carcass up the nest for the workers. I think of rotting carcass, gross ... but keep following these two. We come to a cavern which seems a bit dingy and run down. I am a bit wary. I am looking into what seems to be an eye, but it was hard to tell – was it a spider?

Then I am in a room with some cats, I see a lamb too. It comes to me and I pat it. In the room, photos and memories come to mind. I notice I see only the negative aspects of life. I am then in a grass field. A pumpkin shaped balloon is let go and floats up into the air.)

V: Let go.

(The balloon is the negativity I see. It is hard, but I say)

A: I want to let go. Help me let go.

(In the grass I am approached by Tiger and a lioness. Other tigers and lions walk towards me and surround me in a circle. A lioness comes right up to me and puts her paws on me and licks my face. Then she lays facing me on the ground ... the others do too. I then realise I must allow myself to be dismembered and eaten – to be renewed. I hesitate.)

Li: You must.

(A woman surrounded by many animals came alongside and said)

WW: You must.

(I think she was the wild woman of a previous active imagination. I consented and my face is eaten, my stomach is eaten, arms, legs torn off. I am not really aware of this happening. I kind of had no body and had an existence apart from the body. After this I begin to grow. I do not know what I am. I was not human, but I am some animal. After a while I begin to think I am a bear. I felt awkward and stumbled around.)

V: Learn how to be a bear.

(At some point in time Bearman, from an earlier dream, would join me and teach me how to be a bear.)

In this largely narrative encounter two years later, the theme of the earth continues to be important. Here Ann finds herself drawn into the earth. She begins by floating above Tiger and the scene, but ends up on the earth and then in the earth. She enters a cave, follows ants crawling in the soil, ends up in an ants' nest with the eggs, again in a cavern, and finally in a room with animals again. Then in a field, she lets go of a balloon that represents her tendency to see negative thoughts. Finally she is encircled by tigers and lionesses and endures being dismembered by the lionesses. She is both in the experience and observing it. From this she arises as a bear, and realises she will learn how to be a bear from the Bearman from a previous dream.

The number of animals in this experience is unusual, and suggests that Ann's task involves becoming more attuned to the animal, earth bound aspects of her own being. Each may represent some part of her emerging feminine consciousness. The dismemberment experience stands in the shamanic tradition. The vocation of the shaman in some cultures often was revealed to the individual through a ritual dismemberment dream or vision. Ann's experience also has the death and resurrection cycle from her faith tradition as a key reference point. From the experience Ann emerges and senses herself now to be a bear who will need the guidance of the Bearman to explore this identity. This narrative experience brings her a long way from floating above Tiger in the opening scene, right down to the earth and the instinctual, animal aspects of her emerging sense of being woman.

Geoffrey's Dream and Dialogues

Geoffrey is a mental health professional in his early 60s. He is married with grown children and a grandchild. He lived much of his earlier life in Africa. He was confronted rather suddenly with a need for a major medical intervention. He knew this medical event represented a much deeper need for change in his life in addition to the medical procedure. Shortly after the medical experience, and during his rehabilitation, Geoffrey had the following dream. This led to his undertaking the two active imagination dialogues.

The Dream: I am unsure of the context but somehow there was a dead impala ewe. I think I was meant to pack it away or something. There were people around – maybe some sort of market. The impala stood up and everyone was horrified. I tried to put its head in a pot under a cloth to get it to lay down (not be seen). When I checked, I had put its head in boiling cooking oil. I was beyond horrified and woke up thinking of the incredible pain I had inflicted on this poor animal. I feel quite distressed and an element of self-loathing. "How could you be so stupid!!!" It feels like I made the mistake because I was under pressure to cover up the fact that it was still alive. This has left me not feeling good!!!

1. Me: me; Persona: P.

Me: What are you doing?

P: I'm forcing the impala to lie down so it won't be noticed.

Me: Why?

P: It's meant to be dead. It's not meant to be alive.

Me: What happens if it's alive, if it's seen.

P: I'll be in trouble, I'll be judged. People expect the impala to be dead.

Me: So why did you cover its head?

P: So it wouldn't be noticed. So it would be still – look dead. Not draw attention.

Me: But you killed it very brutally in hot oil.

P: That was a mistake. I didn't want it to suffer. I just wanted it to be dead, or look dead, so that no one would notice.

Me: What are you afraid of?

P: I fear people will judge me for having a live impala in a market. I may be in trouble. I may be chucked out.

Me: What would you do differently?

P: I don't know – I just know what I did was not ok. When I saw it was alive, I did see how beautiful it was, but told myself it would die anyway.

Me: Why?

P: It seemed so gentle and frail.

Me: Can you let the impala live and take the consequences?

P: It will cost – maybe a great cost, but Yes!

2. Me: me; Im: Impala.

Me: Who are you?

Im: I am the very best of you – your beauty, your gentleness, your depth. I am your loving, caring, generous, giving feminine.

Me: My anima?

Im: Yes, but more! I am beyond your narrow restrictions of male and female. I am wild and free, I am your soul.

Me: But I am not opposed to my inner feminine.

Im: (almost laughing) You say the right things, but practically, socially, you shut me down, chain me, hide me. It seems I embarrass you.

Me: Really – I do that?

Im: Who do you show weakness to? – very few. Who do you share you're your deep spiritual beliefs with? Anybody??? Who do you share your desperate desire to commune with God with??? You deny your soul, you deny me – you hide me, sometimes it feels as if you want to kill me.

Me: That's terrible, but true. How much damage have I done?

Im: That cannot be quantified but needs to stop. I showed myself as an impala as you know this animal so well. So many hunting trips yet you never shot a female impala. You preserved them, you loved them. You saw their strength, their speed, their agility, their resilience. You always cared – Embrace me, show me, delight in me, and I will flourish as the herds of impala did under your care.

Im: It's not too late, but start today, start right now!!!

Me: I commit to loving you, to honouring you, to not hiding you – in fact to be proud of you. I will serve you as you lead and guide me – as you flourish.

Geoffrey concluded with: "Amen," and added this statement, "Love has the final say of who I am." In his further reflections Geoffrey states, "I don't trust my inner feminine. I always suspect it will get anxious, implode, react – let me down. I see this so clearly now. I let my inner feminine 'out of the cage' when it's safe but very quickly hide it if it is going to be seen. I think I project this onto (partner) too. She's dependable, but I never want to be dependent!"

Geoffrey's projection onto the impala as a symbol of his soul sets clearly the agenda for his life after his medical episode. The impala here is a female for which he had significant admiration and respect for many years. He knew he was in for big changes because of the medical experience, and the dream and dialogues affirm this intuition. It is clear that his understanding of masculinity from his earlier years will no longer serve him well and could be dangerous if he does not now pay close attention to this new experience of soul wisdom. The impala is more than can be described by the technical term "anima." She declares, "I am beyond your narrow restrictions of male and female. I am wild and free, I am your soul." She implies that he knows her intellectually, but not as a vital inner experience. "You say the right things, but practically, socially, you shut me down, chain me, hide me. It seems I embarrass you." It is interesting to note that, in his initial reflection, he refers to the feminine as "it," rather than "she." Yet the impala herself declares that she is beyond these gender descriptions. The impala challenges Geoffrey to live from, and learn to trust, this deeper life of the soul. This challenge prompted Geoffrey to extend his recovery time away from work, and to travel into the bush for a significant time in retreat alone for prayer, reflection and writing.

George's Dream and Dialogue

I have chosen two dialogues of my own to share. The first of these took place in 1977, and the second in 1988. While they are eleven years apart, they address the same theme. Sometimes I think I am a slow learner. It seems I take years to get the message, or perhaps I need to engage the deeper issues of my life more than once in different ways, and in different contexts. However this may be, the two dialogues address a common theme.

I undertook the first dialogue after a dream in which a grizzly bear appeared and was tearing up a landscape much like the Garden of Eden. My analyst at the time, Weyler Greene, suggested that I might find it helpful to speak with the bear, and I resolved to do so. As I indicated in the Introduction, this was among my earliest experiences of active imagination. It is the experience that convinced me of the value of these dialogues as a way of dealing with my inner life.

In my young adult years I received the diagnosis of a back condition that was from birth. Surgery has never been suggested as a viable option, and I have variously lived with a brace, medications and ongoing advice to exercise. (I swim, I walk, I grizzle.) Pain has been an ongoing companion over these decades. In 1988, when I was in another city leading a retreat/conference over several days, I was experiencing considerable pain. I decided to take my own advice and set up a conversation with my back. I wanted to see if there was anything I could do to help ease the pain. I knew intuitively that the pain was not just a physical issue; something psychic was amiss. The dialogue with my back was an important and life-altering encounter. I will say more about this second dialogue as a preface to it. Both of these dialogues were deeply significant for me. Each encounter caused me to reflect on my conscious point of view and to work for change. We start with the dream.

Dream: The Grizzly Bear

> *I am looking on a scene as pleasant and idyllic as the Garden of Eden. In the garden I see two animals, like antelopes, beautiful and sleek. They are about to join together sexually, when I hear a great roar from off in the bushes. Suddenly out of the undergrowth comes a great grizzly bear reared up on his hind legs. He is huge and growls ferociously. He is intent on tearing up the garden and attacking the two animals. I am frightened and wake up. I am very agitated on waking.*

1.
Dialogue: G: George; GB: Grizzly Bear.

(I replay the dream from the beginning and enter the scene when I see the bear begin to rip into the garden.)

G.   Stop that! Who are you? What are you doing?

(The bear stops and looks down at me.)

GB   I am your anger!
G.   Grizzly bear, I'm really afraid to confront you.

GB: Why? I only do what is natural.

G. I am terrified of your strength and energy; I could never win against you.

GB. I only hurt those who try to abuse me; treat me right and I'll never hurt you.

G. It's hard to trust that, I'm not accustomed to such strength, such passion; when you growl and show those teeth, I shudder.

GB. Well, that's who I am, I can't be any other, and I have no need to hurt you if you treat me fairly. Actually I'm not all tough and rough noise; I'm playful and fun loving as well.

G. It's hard to remember any other side of you when I see your ferocious side. Would you have killed those animals?

GB. Look, I'm natural; I eat by killing, that may be hard to accept but it's true. Remember the law of nature that governs who I am.

G. But those two – they seem significant to me.

GB. Okay, those two I won't hurt for you. But you are going to have to come to grips with me; who I am and how I live. I really mean you no harm, but I won't tolerate being abused; then I'm <u>really</u> ferocious.

G. Okay, I'll do my best to see you from both sides.

GB. All right, and I'll withdraw so your animals can find each other.

G. See you again.

GB. You bet you will.

(After the grizzly bear withdrew I saw the two animals come together. They became human beings, a man and woman, engaging in sharing love. I was both of them and felt the experience as first one and then the other.)

This dialogue challenged me to acknowledge more honestly my capacity for anger and to realise that it is triggered by a variety of circumstances. Some of these are of my own doing and others come to me from the normal and complex events of life. What began to be clear was that my attitude toward the daily events of life was critical to the health and well being of the Garden, the landscape of my life. I was challenged by the bear to cultivate a positive and attentive relationship to my anger, and thereby to create a more wholesome and inclusive connection with myself.

The dialogue with my back now moves our attention from animals to parts of our bodies. I have two examples of such encounters. This dialogue with my back is part of a series of sixteen dialogues that I undertook with an Old Nun who appeared in a dream. This is the twelfth dialogue in that series. As I entered the experience, I spoke with her and with the old Monk who helped me settle down. When I have no dream image to work with I imagine standing before a fog or heavy shadows in which the one I am seeking is present. I then address this opaque space and ask the other, in this instance my back, to assume a form with which I can converse … and then I wait. The dialogue that followed in this instance was quite long. I have, therefore, summarized the encounter with a combination of narrative and dialogue that I hope retains something of the energy that was in the experience.

2.
Dialogue with my back. G: George; B: back.

G.   My back, take your image, reveal yourself to me. (Soon I hear sounds off to my right, moans, low groaning, labored breathing.) Is it you?

B.   Yes George, It is I! (He weeps as he speaks.)

G.   You are crying.

B.   Yes, of course! Look at me buried under this mound! Look at me!

(I look and see an older man, with sparse hair, buried in rubble above his waist. He looks like someone caught in a bombed building.)

G.   Back? My God, is it you?

B.   Yes! (He yells at me.) Look at me, mired down in all this rubble, all these cares and concerns, all these senses of responsibility; God! It's no wonder I ache; It's a miracle I can walk at all. How could you do this to me? (He is crying.) Look at me, George, for God's sake, what have you done? Help me out of this!

G.   What have I done? How did I do this? Here, let me help, careful now.

(I begin to pull.)

B.   It won't do, you can't yank me out. Start digging, with your hands!

G.   It will take forever!

B.   Dig! Dig me out; you got me in!

G.   What have I done?

B.   I'm your rubble heap, George. I'm where you dump all the things you fear to face, or that you only half perceive. I'm it kid; whenever you can't deal with something, or lack courage to confront, or feel powerless, it all gets s**t canned in the back. Stone after stone, barrow loads, pebbles, it all comes on me. God, how could you?

G.   I guess I realised it in some way, but I didn't mean to; I didn't understand it was like this.

B.   Can't you feel? How insensitive are you? Can't you feel? Who in the hell has been crying in pain? Are you that out of touch? I am you! This is your back speaking!

G.   I don't know what to say.

B.   Dig!

(I begin to dig stone by stone. They are endless and of all sizes.)

G.   Does each stone represent a different event or something?

B.   That's coming out of your head! Dig! Together they represent the unfaced life. To be fair some represent more important things than others.

(So I dig.)

G.   I'm sorry; I don't know what else to say, but I am sorry. I really don't know what to do with so many of my feelings that I guess I dump them all.

B.   Keep talking, show me you aren't completely insensitive.

G.   Ok – I know I don't know what to do with a lot of my anger.

B.   Tell me about it!

G.   No news to you I see.

B.   Hardly. Talk about it.

G.   Well. I know I'm angry at lots of people. I feel too responsible, and sometimes too depended upon; but I don't know what to say, so I say nothing.

B.   But you do something. You dump on me!

G.   Okay, I admit it. I just fear confrontation and dialogue. I fear hurting or confusing people.

B.   It's deeper, George.

G.   It has to do with being super-responsible?

B.   Deeper yet.

G.   It has to do with the fear that people won't love me if I'm not Mr. Dependable.

B.   That's more like it. The anger and frustration get dumped on me because you fear that love is conditional. You still can't believe that people can simply love you.

G.   I guess that's true. I see myself programmed to buy love by being Mr. Someone for others. I guess I've always felt like I had to perform, function in a splendid way so I'd be loved.

B.   George, are you aware that this is the dark side of all the "brilliant teaching?" You are out buying love. You are out performing like the organ grinder's monkey, and killing me!

G.   I don't know where to go from here.

B.   Keep digging, notice that you see more of me?

(I realise that I've taken away enough stones to see his waist and hips. In digging him out I name other long held angers and wounds of the past … with my faith tradition … with the experience of feeling betrayed)

B.   Partly that's your fault, you didn't push.

G.   Courage, I really lack courage.

B.   Yes, in a way you're a wimp.

G.   Hang on!

B.   Well, it's true. You frequently back down, or agree or murmur assent or interest in order to avoid unpleasantness or confrontation. It's wimpy and guess who suffers?

G.   So I see.

B.   It isn't enough to see, George, it has to change. Keep digging.

(... Then came anger with people who offer unsolicited advice concerning my back ... feeling like the organ grinder's monkey, here to please ... being the good boy for the family – doing all the right things by them ... carrying my own problems secretly so as not to upset others ... sometimes wanting to say or do something hurtful to the family almost as payback ...)

G.   S**t, I don't know what else to day. Can't I just pull you out?

B.   No. Dig. How are you and old God in all this?

G.   Clever you, hit hard don't you.

B.   Like a stone, bucko, dig.

G.   Well, yes, I really don't know how to be angry at God, but I am. Oh, I can get mad, righteously over world problems and the like, and that's good; it makes me think we've got such a good relationship. But I am angry about me! What the hell, I've had to carry a s**t can load of stuff.

B.   You?! Look at me!

(Here came the listing of some of the wounds of childhood and the younger years ... single parent home, financial insecurity, absent father, distant brother, and a serious illness ... painful teen years ... and loneliness ...)

G.   Why did all this have to happen? Did I lose the cosmic lottery? Continual fears, fears of rejection ... Then the back – ah the back – nothing like striking down the young! What can I say, you know all about this one.

B.   Yes, I do. I am he, and it's been a painful history. And not all of it is stuffed down junk. You got dealt a tough hand.

G.   Yes, I did; and at times it has been really hell – really, really, hell. How many times I've been desperately afraid with no one to turn to; no human face of God. Yes, I am deeply angry for this one, deeply angry. It seems like such a cruel joke. I look good, can act okay, and then, boom! down I go. One wise old woman analyst called you a friend – you, back; and it isn't you I hate, but God; God I hate you for making me carry this one; it seems do damned unfair.

B.   Can you go on? Keep digging.

(The angers, challenges and wounds of the middle years ... alcoholism, depression, ongoing limits and pain,

G.   Yes, I am angry at God for all this! ... Yes, I love God, whatever that means, but I am angry at God; there is still the "Why?" all the whys, and never an answer. Is this what it is to be human?

B.   For some – at least for you.

G.   Recently I've had moments of envying an old friend as he dies. He gets out of so much. I've really had flashes of envy.

B.   That's not the way out for you, kiddo, that much I know.

G.   Clairvoyant?

B.   Close to the source.

G.   Oh.

B.   Any stones left to take away?

G.   Well, yes. I've also dumped on you anger at myself. Part of this is self-induced through conditioning. I really believed all those years that I had to be the good guy and hated me

142

when I wasn't. So I've tossed rubble on you for that. But I've also hated me for who I am because I cause myself pain. I've hated the complexity of myself; the complexity of my feelings. I've hated my fears, weaknesses, cowardice; I've hated my unbridled strength, Napoleonic power. It's been hard to come to love me, and I'm not sure I'm even close.

B.   You're doing better, George, much better. So here we are. The stones are enough removed so that I can walk.

G.   So it is.

B.   Look at me.

G.   I am, I am.

B.   George, I am free from the stones, but look and see that I am crippled. Even free from the rubble, I'm not perfect. I, you, am a marked man. It's one of the things you are angry, frustrated and powerless about. Even when things are clear and the rubble is minimal, I'll have some struggles. But you can keep it minimal if you try to look at the rubble you throw here.

Yes, you have lots to deal with, lots to carry; in some ways more than others, in some ways less. What matters now is that you take full responsibility for the share of the work that is yours. It will go much better if you do. The simple beginning is to connect with it all – you can't make it all okay on the outside, but the honest facing of the feelings of anger, frustration, powerlessness, fear, will be a good beginning.

You are blessed with an unusual and supportive inner family; ask them for help in carrying things. You are older now on the outside, and now mortal. What time is left to you can be very good; you need not fear. Try daily to be aware of what you feel, even write it if necessary; trust the inner ones to support you and look for ways to relate more completely to the outer family; that will allow you to feel supported and free. Thank you for uncovering me. Now you can get well.

G.   Thank you, back. I just wonder if I really grasp any of this.

B.   Grasp it – you've lots to think about – but do it.

(The encounter ends in a mutual greeting with the Old Nun and villagers.)

It is difficult to find words to describe adequately the impact of this encounter. The dialogue left me both deeply at peace and deeply unsettled. At first I could hardly accept it, and part of me wanted to dismiss it. I had the feeling that I had acknowledged angers and pains from across many decades of my life experience, and somehow had cleared this out from the depths of my soul. I felt emptied and much lighter, and I was not sure what would come of it. I knew I had done something very significant, and was given much on which to reflect over time. What did happen in the short term was that my pain became more manageable and I was able to change my physical treatment sessions from two a week to fortnightly. I also felt more in touch, and more honest, with myself. The grizzly bear has not made another appearance. I would like to think he roams freely on the outskirts of the village. "Back" on the other hand, is in the village and often is found lounging around on a comfy pallet in the village circle. He is more than happy to tell me if I am abusing him, and to affirm me when things are going well. The distinction he made in this dialogue between our medical condition and the psychic issues of anger are still helpful. "Even when things are clear," he says, "and the rubble is minimal, I'll have some struggles." This has been very liberating. This dialogue has been a turning point in how I accept my body, and exercise care with how "we" live together.

Jim's Dialogues

Jim writes an introduction to his experience that began with stomach pain. "I've been feeling off color for about three weeks, upset stomach, thinking there was some allergy problem with food. Then I started to get mild stomach pain that appeared to get worse. I mentioned the problem to my counsellor during a session, and he suggested I dialogue with the pain in my stomach.

I had been having problems doing active imagination for various reasons. However, I found on this occasion that soon after the suggestion, and during a morning meditation, my mind started to enter a dialogue with my stomach pain. I thought about the old man who would appear soon in my imagination, bent over, clutching his stomach. I shut my eyes and waited for him to appear. Instead, there came a boy, 5 or 6 years old, with a white shawl or blanket around his head and shoulders. This is not what I expected, and I opened my eyes. Over the years I had developed a trust in accepting the first image that came to my mind's eye, but this was so unexpected I thought maybe I wasn't ready, and that I needed to start the experience again. I shut my eyes again. This time there appeared the image of the Christ Child, as an African. So, I said to myself, I was to dialogue with a child and not with an old man."

Jim: J; Little Jim: LJ.

J   Stomach pain, stomach grief, destroyer of my stomach, come to me, assume a figure so that I can talk with you. I sense you come as a young boy. What is this pain, this disturbance, why does it come?

LJ   It comes because I am lost and abandoned. The pain is my grief of loneliness. It is felt more now because of C (my son who was then nearly 3 years old, bright, responsive and affectionate) He reminds you of me, resurrects me in you.

J   But why the grief and the pain? Why do I suffer?

LJ   You don't give attention to me. You rush around, being important and dutiful, trying to impress others. You need to attend to me.

J   How do I do this attending to you?

LJ   It is what you have recently read in "The Cosmic Christ": attending to your 'puer' so to enhance your 'senex' (I think of my work and its pressure and drive). You see, even now your mind wanders onto work! You need to give me space and acknowledgment.

J   I really do not know how to give you space and acknowledgment, other than to be more 'child like'; more trusting and spontaneous. I respect my two children, and give them valuable time – which I love to do – but how to acknowledge you?

LJ   Try to begin to respect yourself.

J   Easier said than done.

LJ   Take your time, you'd achieve as much even if you slowed down.

J   But what has this got to do with acknowledging you?

LJ   Slowing down and being more playful.

J   I'm sure there is something deeper behind it all though. (I feel somewhat impatient and want to get going.)

LJ   You see! Even now you don't want to spend time with me … so I feel lonely again; abandoned, unloved.

J   If I am with my young son and play with him … is this not being with you?

LJ   No, it isn't. There is no one person to replace me – C is C.

J   What ritual should I perform to be able to acknowledge and love you?

LJ   Every day place a flower on my grave.

J   What does this mean? Where is your grave?

LJ   My grave is your soul. Your soul has become shrivelled and dry, but it can blossom and swell with the juice and nectar of life.

J   So, how do I place a flower on your grave, my soul?

LJ   Begin to remember me in your daily meditations, rather than using a mantra.

J   How? How?

LJ   Repeat as your daily mantra, 'Jimmy boy, I love you'. That is placing a flower on my grave.

J   Thank you, Jimmy boy; I now understand, and I will try and remember the meditation throughout the day too.

LJ   Stay with it for a while. You will discover how your soul will grow and mellow to senex.

J   Peace be unto you, Jimmy.

LJ   Peace be unto you, Jim.

This all begins with stomach pain. The child in Jim gets his attention through his body. Little Jim gives him a simple task to draw Jim's attention to this child within. Jim realised that he was trying to resolve issues from his own childhood by attending to his son in loving ways. He realised it was not working, that the two boys,

C and LJ, were not the same, and that he had to address the issues of his childhood separately. He wrote a brief response to his experience. "My stomach pain and general feeling of being off color did go, and I was able, am able, to reduce a sense of anxiety that often comes to me. Remembering, acknowledging and paying homage to the boy in me has been an enriching experience. What adds to the quality is that my own Being has worked out the solution."

It's an interesting parade of animals here, an elephant, black beetle, small bird, little dog, a tiger, lion, impala and a grizzly bear. Each of these for the participants carries a certain association with the energies of the soul, and their appearance in the active imagination dialogues enables us to engage these deep energies of the soul creatively. People in indigenous cultures long have made special associations with their totem animals. In this experience we can make similar associations that enrich our self-understanding and enlarge our capacity to relate, no only to other people, but also to the wider life of creation. The animals as symbols can take us to deeper dimensions of the soul's vibrant energy than our rational minds and language can access and articulate.

It is important to realise that these animal symbols need not be negative. While my grizzly bear was on a rampage, it was only because he was feeling the abuse of neglect. He was otherwise friendly and supportive. This was an important lesson for me about the energy of anger. I now see it more as my passion for life in many forms. When abused or denied, the energy will act up in a negative way. This is also true of our domestic dogs and cats. Mistreat a household pet and it will arc up in defence. It is nature in action. The animals represent nature; it is we who determine the expression of the character of that nature, usually in reference to our present points of view. Once we engage our totem animals, they are remarkable companions in the understanding of our souls and the expression of our lives.

It may be less frequently that we create an opportunity to speak in dialogue with our bodies. I am convinced it is happening a good deal of the time. I had an amusing conversation with a friend at lunch during the time of writing this chapter, in which I was explaining the experience of dialoguing with our bodies. Out of my assumed sense of wisdom, I spoke as if this was an unusual experience only now understood in the context of active imagination. My companion simply responded, "I do that all the time." He lives with a physical condition that requires disciplined attention and, when he gets careless, his body "speaks" clearly to him as to what it needs. Perhaps what we have in active imagination dialogues is a more structured experience of having these conversations, in which we otherwise participate informally much of the time. What matters is that we make use of these experiences in order to enlarge our self understanding, to strengthen our sense of personal authority and to create a more wholesome life experience. In our next chapter we continue to explore dialogues that assist us in shaping lives with meaning and depth.

CHAPTER FIVE

Encounters with Sacred Images

Deep with us all there is an amazing inner sanctuary of
the soul, a holy place, a Divine Center, a speaking voice,
to which we may continuously return.
Thomas Kelly

When was it that we saw you ...?
Biblical book of Matthew 25:37

In this chapter we engage several active imagination experiences that involve specific sacred images. In chapter three I affirmed that, for many, the experience of active imagination is sacred regardless of the imagery, and I affirm that this can be so for anyone of any or no faith orientation. My experience in the realm of such imagery is limited to people who have had a relationship with the Christian story. Here we engage the images of the Christ, of God and of the Voice. At the time of these experiences, some of those who share here were active in a faith community, and others were no longer aligned with a specific way.

The issue highlighted by these active imagination encounters is the distinction between the traditional imagery of the Christ and of God in the collective faith community, and the individual images of the Christ and God that emerge in personal work. I have found Jung's psychological work of great help in creating a framework for this issue. As I understand Jung's work, he made a clear distinction between the Christ and God images of the faith community, a theological frame, and the individual images of the Christ and God as these appear in the experience of the individual, a psychological frame.

It seems impossible to make a complete separation between the two, as the collective images of the Christ and God found in the sacred texts, and revered over time by the faith tradition, inevitably act as a backdrop, or frame of reference, to some degree, for the individual experience. In terms of the Christ, while we are able to speak of the separation of the historical person of Jesus from the Christ function, the historical Jesus and the amplified Jesus images of the tradition, will continue to inform our understanding of the Christ to a significant degree. As I understand Jung's perspective, the Christ of the tradition, and the Christ of our active imagination encounters, are both expressions of the archetype of Christ that emerge in countless forms from the deep, collective unconscious. Likewise, the images of God in the sacred texts and from the tradition, and the God images that appear in the imagination dialogues of individuals both draw their energy from the deep source of the divine life that enlivens our souls. To see the common ground for these images, enables us be open to engage these images in an endless variety of expressions.

It seems true to affirm that the psychological expressions of these sacred images appear to individuals in direct response to personal need. The unconscious psyche, active within the individual, constellates images of the Christ and of God that correspond with individual need at a particular time.

Many years ago a woman shared her distress in this regard. She had entered into a deep meditation experience and in that "place" came to realise that her divine companion there was not "he," but "she." "She" was more an abiding sense of Presence than a clear image, and it unnerved her in terms of her faith community affiliation at that time. On reflection she was able to affirm that this sense of Presence was what she needed for her own growth, even though it was a sense of Presence that was clearly outside the faith tradition in which she had been living. The core concern here is to consider how to engage an image that connects to the sacred tradition, but that is different in appearance or attitude from that which we have known from within the tradition. What do we do when the sacred images of the soul challenge us to expand our understanding of the divine presence?

In order to engage what may be unconventional sacred images, it is essential to move our attention beyond traditional appearances and attitudes to the notion of function. To stay specifically with the Christ image, what are the functions of the Christ? In Jung's frame, what is the function of the Christ archetype? When we sort out an understanding of the function of the Christ, we are more able to assess the images that come through the active imagination encounters.

From my point of view, I affirm, from the texts and the tradition, that the Christ as manifest in Jesus, functions to liberate, to heal, to challenge and to connect people to the divine life in the depth of their souls. The Christ of the texts challenges people to social responsibility, and loyalty to the truths of the soul before our commitments to any social, faith, and economic or political system. We are challenged to choose the paths of compassion, forgiveness, love, peace, justice, mercy, and to affirm all life as sacred. This Christ of the texts and the tradition challenges people to engage the path of wholeness and completeness. The Christ of the texts and tradition invites people into a conscious, intimate, and ongoing relationship with the divine life. Once we can focus on the various functions of the Christ, we are able look beyond appearances to benefit from our individual and some-times unusual encounters.

The world of visual art can provide us with help in this reflec-tion. Visual images of the Christ have been shaped over countless years in the forms of local cultures of many peoples across the globe. Many pictorial anthologies of Christ in art include images of Christ as Indian, Asian, Indigenous, and African, and these local, cultural images allow people to engage the function of the Christ more deeply. In a sense it seems essential that the images of the Christ archetype need to be framed in local forms in order for the function to be engaged in a meaningful way. This is the key point here in reference to the individual images that emerge in active imagination. Using the frame of visual arts, we can affirm that these internal images are Christs, who have come in "local" appearance in order to meet the needs of individuals, that is, to function as the Christ for their souls. As I reflected on this, I remembered an incident from my work in the early 1970s. I was co-teaching a high school unit with a colleague who was a Roman Catholic priest. In one on his presentations he stated that the Christ was more than Jesus. This is affirmed in the notions of the pre-existent Christ present with God from the beginning. Jesus is one expression and a central one, of the eternal Christ energy, the archetype. This theological interpretation paves the way to see distinctions and differences between Jesus of Nazareth and archetypal expressions of the Christ.

The separation of the Christ function, the archetype of the Christ, from the historical person of Jesus, opens the way for people of the faith tradition to understand more freely the challenge to imitate Christ. Marie-Louise von Franz comments in one place that the imitation of Christ does not mean that we are to "ape Jesus," but to seek to act in the spirit of the Christ, the Christ function, in our own times and places. Our attempts to do this reveal that we are consciously or unconsciously separating this archetypal Christ function from the person of Jesus in order to be Christ-like in our own lives.

Here in the practice of active imagination we are focused on engaging images that express the Christ function, even if the appearance and attitudes of the image are significantly different to the traditional images of the faith. These introductory reflections are meant to enable us to create a framework in which we may engage and honour the following dialogues with images of the Christ that differ from the usual images of the faith tradition.

Ed's Dialogues

We met Ed in chapter three through two dialogues. These two dialogues here took place about the same time as the other two. Ed was raised in a conservative Christian community, and struggled from late childhood forward to find a way to fit in because he came to realise he was gay. He also found that the public persona expected of him required him to repress much of his inner life that was seen in his faith and family cultures as negative. This set him at odds with himself, and the result was that he was trying to be too good for his own good. In these dialogues Ed encounters the one he calls the "Swearing Jesus." This Jesus, the Christ, is well outside the parameters of the tradition he has known. He found himself intrigued by him, not put off, just not sure what to make of this Jesus. In an earlier encounter before these two dialogues Jesus had appeared in Ed's village square. He wore only a loincloth, was dragging his cross over his shoulder, and was swearing. The exchange between them was very brief. It was as if Jesus was making an introductory appearance. We then come to these two dialogues; I have edited some of the language in the texts.

1. The characters are Ed, Ed; and Jesus, J.

(I'm in the square sitting by the fountain. I can hear a dragging noise but cannot see yet what it is. I then see swearing Jesus appear on the edge of the square with his large wooden cross over his shoulder and dragging on the cobblestones. He walks slowly and the cross bounces over each cobblestone. He arrives at the fountain, puts the cross down leaning against the fountain ledge and sits beside me with a large sigh.)

J: "That cross is a f*****g heavy b*****d.
Ed: (I nod.) Hi.
       (He looks at me a little oddly and just nods at me.)
Ed: I've been thinking a bit lately about how or what to do, re-engage with the spiritual and religious aspects of us. From personal stuff through to group and church kind of things. So I thought I would come and ask what your thoughts are on such things.
J: F**k ... (He pauses. He appears baffled by the question.) "Well, it would be great to be able to talk to people about Jesus and s**t. I don't have much interest in going to church, that hasn't really been all that effective, in hindsight. I love conversations with people that can be intellectual and academic but also passionate and emotional, which

I suppose might be a tough f*****g ask. But there you go, that's something that I would like. We've never been particularly symbolic with religion, but I think there might be some useful s**t there. But really targeted stuff, not time wasting crap. It's great to be able to hang out with people, and not even talking about God or Jesus, but do normal s**t, but to be around people that, you know, think and act similarly. I liked it when we lived with the guys, particularly M and T, that you could just casually talk about God without any explanation required, that was cool. I know we are studying sustainability, which I think is f*****g awesome, but is there something we can do on the social side of things, like some volunteering, not to preach or "witness" or that kind of train wreck from our past, but just to help people, not for some payoff but because its good for them and good for us? It's like taking care of the words and the deeds, thoughts and actions."

Ed: That sounds good, thanks for sharing with me.

J: Oh its a f*****g pleasure I can assure you. (He gives a big smile.)

Ed: Anything else, or particular details for how this might work?

J You see that big f*****g wooden cross. I've gotta drag that b*****d wherever I go. Over every one of those s**t f*****g stones. How about some bitumen in this village, hey how about you imagine some of that s**t up. Anyway, I think I've done enough, you don't get it all handed to you on a f*****g plate. You're a resourceful lad, I'm sure you'll come up with some ideas.

Ed: Ok, thanks for your thoughts.

J: No worries, take care of yourself.

2. The characters are: Ed, Ed; Jesus, J; Boy, B.

(I arrive in the square and Jesus arrives at the square, he does not have his cross with him today.)

Ed: Hello.

J: Hi.

Ed: I wanted to ask you, if you would come with me to the jail to possibly talk to someone there?

J: Yep, sure thing, let's go.

(We walk to the jail, enter it and descend the stairs into the darkness. I switch on the torch I have brought and shine it down the corridor. The first door remains open and the three other doors remain locked.)

Ed: I've tried talking to the person or persons in the second cell, but they seem very agitated and they've not responded to me verbally. Do you think, as an agent of reconciliation you might be able to try?

J: S**t, that sounds a bit fancy, whatever that is. But yeah I'll give it a go.

(I offer him the torch but he shakes his head. He walks slowly past the first door and as he approaches the second door the rattle noise begins, though much more softly then before. He walks up to the door, grabs one of the bars with his hand.)

J: Hey, how you doing?

(There is a crash against the door and Jesus is bumped back away from the door by the force.)

J: Ok, so that didn't work so well.

(He steps back closer to the door, but still a metre or two from it.)

J: "Look mate, I'm not sure who you are, or what your story is,
        but I can tell you now that whatever you have to tell, there
        are people here that will care about you and your story and
        who long to see you back with the rest of us, trying to make
        a life, making heaps of mistakes, but getting there eventu-
        ally. So if you want to tell me a bit about your story I'd be
        happy to listen, or if you don't, I'm happy to just stand here
        and look stupid. At a guess I'd say you've had a pretty s**t
        time, I imagine people don't end up in here for no reason,
        somebody saw you as unsafe or unmanageable, but I'd say
        things were a bit different when that happened. Maybe now
        you would find those with the keys a little more under-
        standing and desiring that all the parts of us are together."

(From the cell comes the voice of a teenage boy)

B: He locked me up, he's the one.
J: Yep, he's done a bit of that. But this cell next to you, it's
        now empty, because he let them out. Now I don't speak
        for him, but really, I tend to think actions speak louder
        anyway, and that empty cell says more than anything
        you'd probably want to hear him say.
B: How can I trust him? He locked me up. I did nothing
        wrong. I was 14 and in a lot of pain and he locks me up.
        How is that explainable or even forgivable?
J: Well its probably explainable in some psychological s**t,
        but who gives a f**k about that. At a heart level its pretty

f*****g hard to explain … and to forgive … well how do you do that, not easily I reckon. But that's the really unfair part, that if you don't forgive then you may as well not be in this cell, cos you'll be locked up in your own cell of anger, you'll be the one to lose the most from it.

B: I was fourteen and everything that I knew was ripped away from me. I didn't get any choice, I was sent off to [city] and I hated it. I was so alone and didn't know how to make friends. Day after day I would go to school and have no one to talk to. Night after night I would come home, have dinner, watch TV and go to sleep and have no friends to talk to. I tried to talk to Mum and Dad, but that cost a fortune on the phone, which they had to pay and I felt bad about that. I cried most days and that chest pain that everyone is getting so upset about now, well that was there just about everyday for years. I didn't have any valium, I didn't have a psychologist to talk to, I didn't have an income to pay for the phone calls, I didn't have any friends, there was no where I could go, I was in a big city for the first time and everything was scary, I dressed in clothes and shoes that people would laugh at cos I had no clue about fashion. I had to rely on my sister to take me places, but she had her own life and worries and stupid boyfriends that didn't want me around. Nana would pick me up and I could go to her place, which was a great thing for her to do, but its not exactly what a 14 year old boy wants to be doing. I spent years with no one to talk to and no one that understood what I was going through. I tried so hard, to make friends at church and youth group but I think they found me boring because I was too shy and didn't have a clue what to talk about. I was too scared of saying something stupid that I said pretty much nothing.

It was really, really horrible. And after all this, I get put in here to rot and fester. I could have been and done lots of things, so many exciting possibilities in life, but I go through all that, pushing me down and then I get put in here so I can't do anything but slowly die. I don't want to be angry, I don't want revenge I want to go back to the start and for it to be different. I don't [want] to be just let out of here so that I can fall flat on my face all over again, I would rather die. There is only one thing I want, to go back to being 14 and live a different life."

(There is silence for a bit.)

J: Thank you for sharing that, that's very heavy stuff and I'm saddened to hear what you've been through. I really wish that had not been the case. I also think it was unfair that after all that you were locked up down here. I can't change what has happened in the past and I can't change what will be in your future, but I do believe that your future can be very different and much better than your past.

B: I don't want a future, I just want to go back and for it to all be ok, for it to go the way it should have in the first place, where I'm not lonely and I'm not a loser. That is all I want and if I can't have that then I want to die.

J: Well I respect what your wanting here. I can appreciate to some degree why you don't have much faith in life here and now. But what if both of your two options are not possible? What then?"

B: Well then I'll stay here, I'm not coming out. I'm not going through that again. If your not going to help me then just leave.

161

J: Well leaving people that are hurting is not really my style. To be honest I don't know what might happen if you were to come out. I'm not going to tell you some rosey s**t about life being wonderful and full of butterflies and rainbows. It's often hard and sometimes painful. However I have seen some amazing s**t, right here in this village. I reckon it's amazing that we are even here talking to you. Did you ever think this would be happening?

B: No

J: See, this doesn't mean your future will be perfect or without pain, but it does show that great change is not only possible but that great change is occurring all around you. And there is no reason at all, that if it is happening with others why it would not happen with you. No reason at all.

B: I still don't want to. I only want to go back.

J: Ok. Well I'm not going to badger you. I have really enjoyed chatting with you, maybe we can do it again if you would like that?

B: I would.

J: Ok then. So we'll leave you be for now, and I'll come back and chat to you some other time, ok?

B: Ok.

J: Seeya.

B: Bye.

(We walk out of the jail and I thank Jesus for coming with me.)

J: I think he is in some serious pain, I don't think even a small part of it is visible. There is a lot of s**t locked up in that cell.

Ed: Ok.

Ed notes that he did complete this work. The boy did come out of the prison cell, became a part of the village family, and had many conversations with Ed. Ed was awed by the opportunity to engage the 14 year-old boy in his soul, to hear his painful story, and to liberate him from his prison cell. This was very meaningful for him. Swearing Jesus served as a reconciling energy for Ed with the boy, and an encouragement to continue on with the work of liberating the boy from his prison. Jesus functions to encourage Ed to trust himself, to imagine the way forward and to do his work. Jesus says, "Anyway, I think I've done enough, you don't get it all handed to you on a f*****g plate. You're a resourceful lad, I'm sure you'll come up with some ideas." He is invited to initiate action for his own healing and a more wholesome life.

This Christ image, swearing Jesus, functions to break open all the boundaries of repression for Ed. Through his dramatically unconventional appearance the Jesus figure functioned as a balancing compensation for Ed's persona, his attempts to be too good for his own good. Engaging this swearing Jesus was a very liberating encounter. Ed mentioned that he felt given permission to swear when frustrated, and this alone represented a release from the pressure to hold back and to always be good in some superficial sense. Ed was encouraged that Jesus affirmed that he had "seen some amazing s**t, right here in this village." This helped Ed consider that his inner work was progressing, and that it is a long-term work full of promise.

While this encounter with swearing Jesus did not motivate Ed to re-join a Christian community, it has resulted in his being sensitive to the Jesus image, the Christ within, and to his influence on the values by which Ed lives his life.

Graham's Dialogue

The Christ image in Graham's experience also stands outside the usual expectations of the tradition. He was in a time of deep distress, and was finding his religion to be of little help to him. He felt drawn to have a show down with Jesus. He titled his experience, "Fighting with Jesus." It is lengthy and detailed, and I have created a summary that focuses on the interaction with Jesus. I have again edited some language in the text. The narrative at the beginning describes an elaborate scene of a standoff. Both Graham and Jesus arrive at the scene with their minders, ready to fight. It is on a mountaintop, by a lake, and there is a Tree of Life nearby to which Graham nods as he takes his place and waits. The fight begins with Graham rushing forward "in a blind fury," pounding his fist into his hand and screaming curses in Jesus' face. The narrative continues:

"I saw a blur of movement in my peripheral vision and turned my head as I swayed back, but I was a moment too slow and too late. An explosion went off inside my head as Jesus' fist connected with my jaw. I felt like a drunk man falling in slow motion as my knees buckled, I turned, putting out my hands to try to cushion my fall, my eyes couldn't focus, I misjudged the distance, grasped at thin air and crashed hard into the ground as my arms crumpled like matches. Another explosion went off in my head as my face thumped into the ground, but it felt strangely distant as like a man on an operating table counting down the anaesthetic, vague images came and went as blackness drew down her dark veil. As I slowly regained consciousness Jesus bent over me, grabbed me by the scruff of the neck and yelled,"

J: I am sick of your childish s**t! Of you blaming me for every f*****g thing that goes wrong in you[r] life. You come crying to me like a baby when things don't work out, when I fix them, you forget me! If I don't sort things out and leave it to you, you carry one like a baby and refuse to speak to me for ages until you decide you need me again. Well, I'm sick of it you hear me!

(He flung me back and stood up. I slowly came to my feet, ashamed and annoyed, more annoyed than ashamed. My ego was hurt that he got the drop on me! I turned and walked to the tree staggering as I went. Next thing I knew Jesus grabbed my left arm and put it around his neck and put his right arm around my waist to support me. I looked at him.)

G: You got me a beauty, you next to took my head off!

J.   If you hadn't seen it coming I would have!

(We both laughed and walked together to the tree of life, who embraced us both

Tree: It's about time my boys had it out!

(We had a group hug.)

This is an encounter with Jesus, the Christ image, that is another significant challenge to traditional images. Graham was familiar with violence as a way of exerting power over others. He carried a good deal of anger over experiences and relationships of his past. He had also worked his way out of alcohol addiction to sobriety, which revealed his strength in the face of adversity. Graham is a sensitive soul and was drawn to Jesus and the Christ story, yet his anger was very real. In this active imagination experience he is able to take his anger to the Christ relationship in the violent language and action that he knew from his past. Yet the incident is over before it begins. Jesus gets the first and only punch in and knocks him to the ground dazed. He then tells Grahams off for how he has acted. Graham gets himself up and then Jesus half carries him to the Tree of Life. The Tree of Life speaks with a divine voice, and welcomes them into a group hug.

In the fight, Graham is "bested" by Jesus in the "language" on which Graham had previously trusted. The strong implication here is that what Jesus stands for is a language that is stronger than the violence that Graham has known in his past. Graham is met on his own terms. Jesus prevails, challenges their former relationship and initiates reconciliation. This opened Graham up to new and different ways of relating in which the experience of reconciliation with the Christ provided a larger container for his experiences and relationships.

John's Dialogues

John was in his mid-twenties when he undertook this series of active imagination experiences. The dialogues began in response to a dream, and took place over a period of fifteen months. The original dream takes place in an igloo in the Arctic where John has interaction with an old man and woman. John's task from the dream emerges in the first dialogue in the story. He is told that the igloo is "your soul frozen over from years of neglect." The Arctic is the scene of the dream because "The world is a cold place for you. You are yet to discover the warmth of life. You see the world as a bleak and somewhat pointless place...." As a teenager John had realised that his high ideals were not being realised in his world. He was increasingly disillusioned and had yet to find a positive place of meaning for himself. He was aware that he had developed a cynical attitude toward life. The title for this series grew out of the early dream and active imagination. It is "The Warming of the Heart," and represents the task of John's adventure. He was seeking to warm his heart and soul, and to find a way to relate positively to the world.

There are forty-nine dialogues in the series, and a few interlude dialogues with related themes and people. The original dialogues are one hundred and twenty-nine handwritten pages. This includes several images sketched in pen that relate to the content. In the course of this material there are thirty characters and animals that interact with John. Our focus here is on the interaction with the Christ image that begins in dialogue sixteen. We begin with a brief summary of the journey before the dialogues that introduce the Christ image. Sections in the narrative that are from John's original text are in parentheses.

After initial encounters and adventures along the way, John comes to a city. He finds himself in underground tunnels and feels the ridicule of spirits that mock his efforts. He fends off an attack with his sword, and falls to his knees exhausted and vomits.

Ch: Christ; J: John; M: Martha; Sp: Spirit.
16.

(On my knees recovering from vomiting. I lift my head to darkness. I have lost orientation and wield the sword out to touch the wall of this tunnel. I get up and steady myself. The anger returns and I strike the wall. A hole is pierced through and dusty blades of light slash the darkness as my repeated blows open the hole wider and wider. Crying & frustrated, for moments I do not recognize what has happened. Tears of anger become tears of joy as the light reveals the crumbling skull wall and I sense the presence of him. Laying on an altar is the body of Christ. The light emits from him. This is Christ's tomb. I step inside. I am overawed at the discovery. Is this the tomb of Christ? How can this be? I have found where truth lives. I walk around his body. It is perfectly intact. I can feel its warmth. I stop at his head. I touch his forehead. Christ's eyes open.)

J: Oh, I'm sorry.

(Startled, I retreat several steps lowering my head in reverence. It is a reaction I cannot help. He sits up and says)

Ch: Why are you sorry? You must awaken me. I am the way, I am the way.

J: Christ, I don't know what to say. I am afraid to hear you speak and I am overjoyed at finding you. I am afraid you will disappoint me, and I am afraid you will speak the truth.

Ch: Then I will not speak and you should not speak and just let us be.

(This is Christ. My mind begins to race. How do I see him? He appears in robes, he appears in black, he appears in any form I see him. Then I stop and ask myself, "What is the sound of a thought?" Then I hear the thought: I am your Christ you needn't be concerned. I will show you the way, if there is a way. Give your heart rest. I am peaceful at his words.

Then I see the glow that the harpies took and the golden ring around my head. I see him in the sword I carry and in the child, and the diamond he has found.

Standing face to face with him, I breathe in and breathe out, controlled and relaxed. In my breath are the words, I know, I know. I close my eyes leave the ground and sleep.

I awaken. My feet touch the ground from toes to heel. I want to touch him but I am unsure, afraid to. Is this disrespect? He senses my thought, opens his arms and we embrace. I have a sense of home, of safe, of the journey's end, of returning, of relief, of pleasure ...)

Ch: There should be no inhibitions between us. We should be in harmony, balance with one another.

17.

J: You are what I Imagined, totally cool about things. Everything is everything. But you too must have a dark side.

Ch: What do you see in me? What is it that you are looking for? Do you come to find the perfect being and therefore the perfect answer, or do you seek how to be? Is it the real Christ you expect, your childhood Christ or the Christ of self and the Christ that is within you? In many ways we are all one and yet different. But you know this as the mystery of life, the secret of the two sides of the coin. You must find me as I am. Hear me as I am. But do not judge me from something in your past. I have been your past, I have been your future. Most securely I am your present, indeed I am.

J: And so what might you tell me of the warming of the

heart. Tell me of the liberty of my igloo soul from its ice chamber.

Ch: It has begun already. Sweet man, your naiveté, your innocence, shrouds your mind from the truth of your intuitions. The warming of the heart will allow you to embrace the world, to feel it, to experience it. It will put you back in touch with your irrational side and will bring you joy and pain. (I hear the cynic within and I tell him to be quiet.) Yes I am a symbol of the self. I am the Christ within. I am the warming of the heart now that I am alive and recognized. Ask me any question and I will speak the truth.

J: Where is your dark side?

Ch: It is within and without.

(He holds his fists at the pit of his stomach and his clothing changes from white to black to white again.)

J: Should I travel further?

Ch: That is for you to decide, but your quest is found.

J: How can I trust that? Should I not be trialled more?

Ch: As if your trials have not been enough. Many times you could have turned back. You stopped for a time at the mountaintop looking at the city, but you did not return. You came forward. I believe the lesson is learnt. You must push forward when you know not what else you must do.

J: What is your purpose then? What will you do? Teach me. Advise me.

Ch: I am here to speak with you, to guide you, and more still. Your learning will enlighten you yet.

J: Why can't you tell me now?

Ch: As I said, some things do not change. Why do you come to test me? I have already told you I am who I am within. The outside world is a marriage to the inside world. We are not apart but as one. Together we cross realities. So do not be concerned when all is not known.

J: So what should we do now?

Ch: I do not know, speak to me and tell me.

J: I should find the boy and the dogs.

In 21, after other adventures and conversations, John then decides to travel on. Martha, the woman from the igloo, reappears to travel with them. His adventures continue at one point he and Martha discuss the Christ.

J: I would like to find J.C. I think he is angry with me. I want to know if it is true and then why.

M.   He is not angry with you. She laughs again. (She seems amused at my apparent ignorance.) He seeks what you seek. He is frustrated when you push him away. Own him. Recognize him as yourself as the most valuable part of you. He will return but I advise you to wait for him to appear …

As part of the warming of the heart, John faces several encounters that begin with hostility and require him to work for reconciliation and to restore relationships. Most notable is the encounter with the rebel, the one who hates authority. The resolution between them requires a blood sacrifice sanctioned by Christ.

Ch: This sacrifice is what is needed. You ask us why and we only ask that you proceed.

Christ then presents John with a heart shaped stone imprinted with a cross. In 34 Christ and John have a conversation about the warming of the heart.

Ch: I am sorry. The pain of this life for you is in trusting me. Can you trust me?

(He shows me the palm of his hand jiggered with the scar of a wound.)

J: And should I trust this? A historical event with which you may conveniently allay my fears? It's your heart I wish to know, to believe, to trust.

Ch: I am (he says, and more resigned, yet firm) 'I am.'

J: So why would you show me these actions, the phenomema, the devil, the drinking of blood? What do you mean the devil has my soul?

Ch: Your soul is strong, yet caged. The outer world awaits its release. The devil in you, the form of the devil, your nemesis let us call it, still has your soul.

J: And the warming of the heart?

Ch: The courage to take chance, the freedom of spirit. The awe, the inspiration, the joy, the pain, the love, the experience, the life inside yearning to be heard and acknowledged. The belief in one's own self. The beauty of the love is … Do you understand?

(I nod. Christ advises him how to deal with his nemesis.)

Ch: The answer is easy. Follow your heart. Listen to it speak. It will talk gently, softly. You must be patient to hear its voice. Refrain from hearing the drumming of your mind. Find your hearts voice, eyes closed in the darkness of a country road and let its call bring you home to where you belong.

J: Soothing words Christ. And I will try, but the path is dangerous.

John is then prepared for battle and given several items, not weapons, to use in his encounters. The encounters involve time with Noah on the ark for forty days and forty nights. After this, in 39, John then finds himself at his secondary school. Here he meets a tear of flames on the school grounds. It is his teenage self in fiery form. John pleads with him but he remains silent. The encounter continues:

J: I have been on a journey of the warming of the heart. Things have changed. I am a warrior now. You are part of that heritage whether you like it or not. You cannot deny what is. I will not fight you or raise a hand against you. I will not be divided against myself. I ask that you come to me and claim what is yours.

(He appears in human form. I hesitate to step forward to hug him. I offer my arms instead. He comes to me and we embrace.)

J: I can't promise you anything. I don't know what will happen now, but I am so sorry I ever wrote you off. I was stupid. Thank you for giving me a second chance.

After spending time with the boy in several dialogues, John prepares to encounter his final challenge, his nemesis. He pushes through to "another reality," a large room, and confronts an angry and hostile spirit. John identifies the angry spirit as "a spirit of me, lazy, smiling, slightly crazed." The spirit is hostile and ridicules him. John holds his ground against the hostile attitude, and makes his offering.

J: And here a ring, I give it to you. I have only love to offer you. I will not use anger against you.

Sp: You torment me with this gesture of love?

J: No. I have only this to offer you. My discipline is one of love. This is what I will answer to. I ask you to throw off your armour and embrace me. Finish with your rebellion and answer to love.

(Spirit cries, yet seems angry, fearful.)

J: I know with my anger I hide my fear. It is through answering to a higher creed that maybe we can go forth, maybe we can become brothers, maybe we can become one.

Sp: I understand you, but I resist! I resist you! I am here to fight, to lie, to deceive. I will not give over to any such notion of love.

J: Then what will you live for?

Sp: I ... I do not know.

J: I respect your anguish, I respect your hurt. It is deep. The world does not answer us with answers we are accustomed to. I can only see reason in answering it with love. The good for the sake of good is the only way.

The spirit rips off his mask and armour as he falls to the floor.

John recovers his body, but sees his spirit rise smiling "Like an angel at peace. He has the ring on his hand."

Sp: This is the way back. Follow your heart. Temperance with the mind. Follow the creed of love and the good's sake.

John returns to the griffin and the boy and declares that it is over. It is time to return to the city. The city shape is reforming itself into a circle. John comes to the city riding on the griffin with the boy. All who have been part of the journey now greet him warmly. Mounted on the griffin he swings the sword in the air and declares: "The good for the sake of the good." He talks with Christ.

J: And, Christ, what have you to say?"
Ch: I'm glad you're home.
J: I feel I have much to talk with you about.
Ch: And we have time … I have longed to see you here in this place now.

(Yet he seems to be saying more than this physical place.)

J: My cryptic Christ, and what place is this?
Ch: Home. That is all. This is home.

John's active imagination is in the tradition of the hero's journey and is heroic both in content and in his effort. John persevered over fifteen months, and continued to engage the story with no idea as to where it would take him. His cynicism and anger took several forms throughout the story: The cynic who becomes the underground troll, the rebel, the teenaged boy and the Spirit.

All were forms of his response to a world that disappointed and frightened him. John's companions were few: the dogs, the child, Christ, later Martha, and the griffin at the end. The encounters with adversaries seemed endless.

John's Christ image is different from Ed's swearing Christ and Graham's fist fighting Jesus. The relationship is collegial, a relationship of equal give and take. The two share some blunt and robust conversations. Christ here is supportive and challenging, and asks John continually to trust what he does not understand. Christ sometimes claims not to know, and leaves the action in the outside world to John. John must think for himself and take on his own battles. These are sometimes bloody and fierce encounters that wound him. Christ does not do the work for John. He is a presence and companion. John is not asked to submit to Christ, though the cynic comes under Christ's influence. Christ does not take authority over John but travels with him. Christ claims to be the answer to the warming of the heart: "I am the warming of the heart now that I am alive and recognized." John has to do the work in order for the warming of the heart to continue. His scene with the teenaged boy reveals the deep tenderness that lives in John even though it has been clouded over with anger and disillusionment at the outside world.

Christ declares that all the work and effort of the journey has brought him home. The motto of his new life in the city of his soul will be "The good for the sake of the good." It is a motto that ties together the inner and outer dimensions of John's life.

Through this adventure of The Warming of the Heart, John came to a deeper realisation of his own complexity, and of the richness of his inner life. He experienced a greater sense of personal authority and responsibility for his unfolding life. The exchange with Christ at the end tells us there is more to come, more to be done, more to be lived. John says, "I feel I have much to talk with you about." Christ replies, "And we have time. I have longed to see you here in this place now." Thus this part of the journey comes to conclusion.

William's Dialogues

William undertook his dialogues when he was in his forties and during a time of personal difficulty. There are twenty-two dialogues and journal reflections in this series that took place over a period of eleven months. The series is comprised of eighty-four typewritten, singled spaced pages. William functioned as an ordained priest, counsellor and teacher. He struggled with being gay before this orientation was an acceptable part of the public culture. He carried this orientation as a secret and with a deep sense of shame and fear. His family of origin and his faith tradition had not provided any support. He longed for a committed partnership but had not ever established a long-term relationship. William felt deeply wounded by the circumstances of his life. He carried all this as a deep and painful wound, and struggled with low self-esteem and confidence. Coupled with this was his introversion that made it hard for him to fit in comfortably with others except through his professional roles. Within himself William carried a strong, negative image of God as Judge.

William's dialogues and reflections include encounters with Jesus and God. The starting place for this series came through a remark William heard in a presentation that was focused on the question in the Biblical book of Matthew where Jesus asks his followers, "Who do you say that I am?" The speaker suggested that the question could be reversed so that the individual asks

Christ, "Who do *you* say that I am?" William writes: "The pain and hurt in me is that I am afraid he would answer, 'I do not really know.' I feel emptied of self-acceptance, self-assurance, full of self-rejection, self-hate, self-abandonment. I do not like me."

In the first dialogue William decides to take the risk and ask the question of Jesus. This leads to a lengthy conversation that I have edited.

William sees Jesus sitting on the bank of a stream "clothed in a robe and wearing long hair and a beard." Jesus welcomes him.

J: You are coming to talk with me. I know, please come and sit beside me.

Wm: You knew I was coming? Uncanny, or is it the god-power that you have even within my own imagination?

J: I knew you were coming because of the question you posed about me on Sunday. The questions came to me as you posed it. I heard your cry and your pain, and I was waiting for you. That is why I am here.

(There is silence, as if I am the first that must speak.)

Wm: You are waiting for me to ask you the question?

J: The question you wish to ask me is, "Who do you believe that I am," referring to my belief of who you are? I know the question. You know the question, but it does no good for me to respond until you can ask it of me. Is that not part of what hurts you so much now – your inability to be open with another person and to let them into the inside of you? We need, you have need, both of us have need, to create a dialogue to be open to and with one another. But that cannot start from me, as it is your question and your pain that we are discussing. If it were my pain, or my question, then I would need to ask it of you.

(There is silence between us.)

Wm: It is not easy for me to ask. I think, I am feeling, that in the fear of the asking is part of the pain of my life. I just can't handle much more rejection, or even the fear of rejection. *What do you think of me? Who do you say that I am?*

J: You, my friend, are my gay brother, you who have carried such pain and sorrow within you for so long because of your gayness, and because of the fear of the trampling that others would do to you because of your vulnerable feelings. You are my beloved friend; I have watched you as you have grown, and as the pain of self-hatred has eaten away at you and within you, causing you much physical pain, the pain in your gut, by the way, which you deal with now. You have felt very little sense of self-worth from a very early age, from a time, I venture that you do not even realize; the gayness is like fire heaped upon open wounds. And that is all that you can feel. Your hurt is deeper than your gayness, your hurt is part of your gayness, your hurt seems to invade all of you, and in your hurt you reject yourself as not-worth. That is needless from my point of view, you berate yourself for the things which you are and which you love....You are one whom I have loved from the very beginning....You are my friend, and I would not, nor could I because of the love I have for you, reject you for all that you feel within yourself, for your loves and your wants, and your desires and your attractions. How I have watched you through the years of puberty and your

179

teenage years wish that your feelings of sexuality could go away; how I have watched you grope for something out of nothing in your stuttering; how I have watched you fail time and again in athletics, and in friendships and relationships, and wanted to take you by the hand and tell you to stop choosing to be hurt, stop choosing to expose yourself endlessly to losers and failures, trying to rescue the world when you are the one who needs rescuing now.

Wm: But how to rescue me? Where do I begin …?

The conversation considers other relationships, and then moves toward conclusion.

J: … And I think that is where you can begin to find me and where you can begin to find yourself. In the world of your feelings.

Wm: Still, how to begin?

J.:   You have begun, softly, simply, hesitantly, but you have begun. I want you to hear again that I say that you are my beloved friend, gay, alone, hurting but able to live through it to a yet fuller beyond in this life still. I am wanting to see you make that breakthrough.

Wm: I hope it comes soon.

J: I have the feeling it is going to come very soon. You are already beginning to open the doors to making it happen. Not for someone else, not for your clients, or students, or family, but for you. Then the miracle will take place.

Wm: I am feeling much relieved to know who you believe that I am. I am relieved that you have not rejected me or turned me down. I am feeling more at ease over it now. And more at ease with myself for the moment. There is one thing more that I want to ask. In the past, and even now, I have always come to you. Perhaps you have come to me in the figure of a dream as a young man, but I have not heard you walking up to sit or stand beside me and to talk to me, to intervene, as it were, in my life in my active imagination. I need that from you, too.

J: I will do so.

(I get up and walk back to the house. I pause at the steps and look back, the figure is gone now and I am left alone. Just as he said I would be, to begin on my own. It is the aloneness of the path that is so frightening, and so, at times, paralysing. I wonder at myself that I still have the energy to make the steps that I do for each day. There must be something within that drives me forward. That to me is sometimes the greatest mystery.)

This initial encounter with Jesus was a turning point in William's life. Subsequent conversation with Jesus and others in what was becoming his inner village, helped William attend to his feelings more deeply. In the midst of these conversations, the God image took a variety of forms other than the long-standing image of the Judge. In Dialogue eight the conversation with an inner child centres on the experience of happiness that still eluded William. Jesus told him this healing was coming. William responds:

Wm: Oh, God. (The whirlwind comes forward.)
God: You called?
Wm: This is like a Mel Brooks comedy.
God: I made him too.
Wm: Well, at least you gave him a sense of humour that made

him some money. I haven't earned a thing from my pain and aloneness.

God: Correction, you did earn your priesthood, and your counselling license from your pain and aloneness.

Wm: Ok, I stand corrected again. Always. S**t.

God: You want me to s**t?

Wm: No, just a figure of speech.

God: I am good at figures.

Wm: Oh hell, I can't say anything without some image getting stirred ... but thank you God for directing me and teaching me that you have a wry sense of humour.

God: Yours to be sure.

In Dialogue ten William is speaking with Feeling, and God makes a cameo appearance of humour and interrupts the conversation with some nonsensical comic remarks. In Dialogue eleven three new characters are being seated in the Council circle, Bitch, Anger and Victim. Bitch has arrived like a witch on a broomstick with jet-like engine controls. God enters to help Victim. God whirls in and puts an oxygen mask on Victim, pats him on the back and places him between Child and Abandoned.

God: Suck it up, Victim, suck it up, just like they do at 30,000 feet when the cabin pressure goes off, gulp, gulp, gulp. Whoosh, Oh, what a beautiful morning, oh what a beautiful day.!

Angr: As I was saying before God interrupted us again, although he does provide comic relief to this heavy task of yours ...

As the conversation concludes, as Bitch is helped to her place, she is told she has to give up her jet-propelled ways.

God: I'll step in now. I've always wanted to whirl around on a
"Whirlski."

(God takes the propelled machine and whirls around on it.)

God: Another toy, oh joy, oh joy, oh joy.

(And God jets off into the sky around us for a time. We are
laughing hysterically at God the clown who comes to balance us
just when we need it. I lean my head on beautiful Jesus' shoulder,
I hold Feeling in my arms. I am tired again, but here I feel safe
and secure. And I think for the first time in my entire life in these
moments, I sense what it is to be grounded, at peace, Whole.)

The conversation in the Dialogue takes another turn:

Wm: God, are you ever serious?
God: Just look at the last 45 years. Got any questions about
that?
Wm: No, You've been terribly serious in my life, for all of it. I
enjoy your cutting up. But I realized on Saturday morning
that I need a wise and holy man, a sage, to help me at
times. Infinite wisdom.
God: That, too, I can be. But you get deadly serious mixed up
with infinite wisdom. They aren't the same. Wisdom has
life. Seriousness has a kind of judgement ... You don't
need that now. Let's lighten up and I'll be wise and at
times the clown. I enjoy both.
Wm: Thanks.
God: Don't mention.

The dialogues in this series continued to focus on the relationship between Jesus, God and William, and the growing sense of community among the villagers. The dialogue with Jesus at the outset began a process of change for William in terms of self-acceptance from deep within himself. The clowning of God compensated for the overly serious and judgemental image of God. This also freed William to access the humorous side of himself. It was interesting to learn later that he had for a time been involved in a local community theatre group and was known for comedy acting. As time went along, God also took on a serious teaching role, offering the wisdom William was seeking for his life. His overall response to these dialogues was, "This is a God I'd like to get to know." The deep shift in the relationship with God and Jesus for William also gave him courage to offer workshops on spiritual practice to his local AA groups that were warmly received.

George's Dialogue

At times the sacred presence comes as a voice rather than an image. People report that the voice can speak in a variety of ways. The voice speaks at times in dreams, also in active imagination, and in times when we are awake and in a reflective moment or in need of some clear guidance. My dream and dialogue took place a few years ago. I woke in the middle of the night with this dream.

The war is over. People who have been imprisoned by the English and Germans are able to make their way home. They do so with hesitation and slowly, wanting to catch a secret to take back, an event or strategy, something to cover their shame and to justify

their survival. They seem to wade waist deep in grief as they make
their way back home.

I lay awake a long time in the night, first reflecting on the
dream. The reference is to World War I. It was a tragic slaughter
of people on all sides. The grief would have been beyond description across the entire landscape. The first line continued to repeat
in my reflections, "The war is over."

Then the middle night visitations continued on to what seemed
like a different topic. I found myself wondering about the creative
experience in the soul, about the music the composer hears, but
can never duplicate, the painting the artist sees but cannot replicate, the words and phrases the wordsmith cannot capture. With
this came that sense of being both tortured and inspired by the
presence of this creative energy (the muse), tortured and inspired.
After some time of reflection, I got up to engage in an active
imagination. This is the dialogue.

I greet the Old Man who keeps watch over the village and
then enter the village circle. V: Voice; G: George

V: Go ahead, write what I said to you earlier. (and I write) I
        am your Garden of Eden, your burning bush, yes, add the
        still small voice in the cave. I am your belly of the whale,
        include this as well. I am your cross and I am your heav-
        enly Jerusalem. Alpha – Omega – Beginning and End. I
        AM, I am all the moments, images and more, so much
        more, moment by moment.

        And as well your conversations with (neighbour) and
        others on the street – the g'days and hellos. I am all these.
        I am your inspiration, your images of perfection, whole-
        ness, ideals, perfect nonviolence and peace. I am all of

these. I am your I AM, there we have it. Your task is to let my presence inspire you to give shape and form to me in whatever way seems right, appropriate and meaningful. Do not try to copy or replicate me, just do what you do. I inspire you and I am "it", it what you do.

G: I am so grateful, uplifted – encouraged. Thank you.

V: You are more than welcome. Relax and let what you desire take shape as best it can in your world.

G: I can see that I can punish myself by trying to make things perfect.

V: That won't happen. Sit loosely with all this. Let my presence inspire you, leave the perfect in the inner realms where it belongs. You will be less tortured if you can accept my presence to inspire, but not to duplicate or capture. I am not yours; you are mine. This is enough for now. Relax, let it flow into whatever form is best at the time, in the moment, for the message. Relax. Bless you.

G: I am so grateful and I feel relieved of a burden.

V: Good – the war on many fronts is over. Be at peace.

The Voice speaks as the Divine Life, the great I AM. There was no sense of an image with the voice. The opening declaration of the Voice that I "heard" in the middle night reflections, and that I engaged in the dialogue, affirms the continual companionship of the divine life with me. "I am your I AM, there we have it."

The war is over. On reflection, for me the war that has ended was my continued attempts at perfection, both in character and creative expression. Over many years the drive for perfection has been a kind of torture to my satisfaction with my life and accomplishments. I rarely have enjoyed what I have done well, because it has never seemed quite good enough to me. I realised

I have been trying too hard, driven by delusions of perfection and never achieving what I have imagined with the soul's eye. Perfection is an image that has a purpose on the inside, an ideal perhaps that inspires our aspirations. But on the outside the Voice declares, "That won't happen." I need to learn to live with the gap and sit loosely with it. I will continue to be inspired by images created in the soul, and I need to relax, let them flow into whatever forms are "best at the time, in the moment, for the message." "The war is over," continues to be a very moving statement for me. There was a deep sense of relief from this encounter and declaration.

Ann's Dialogue

The Five Petaled Rose

Ann has shared her experiences with active imagination in both chapters three and four. Here she shares a different active imagination experience. In her reflections several years ago, Ann was making a drawing of free form shapes. She turned it to a particular angle and the shapes looked like five petals of a red rose. She decided to stop and address the image of the rose to see what would emerge. She began with her question and reported that the poem arises from a voice responding to her question that seemed to flow spontaneously. It was as if the poem was writing itself.

What are you five petaled rose?

I am you, your deepest desire
Your heart's true centre

Fold back the layers
And you find within you – Love
The secrets of which are available to
All who seek

To gaze within is to be gazed upon
By one who loves and cherishes
All that is made, seen and unseen.
Its treasures are there for all who
Wish to see them

It is like a pearl
Sparkling in the morning
Waiting to be seen and cherished
Glistening bright in the sun
In all its glory
Yelling out to the world
How wonderful it is to be seen
How joyful it is to be loved
By the lover of all things seen and unseen.

I am the rose
The lover of all things seen and unseen
The revealer of hidden things
The cherisher of the gentle heart
The petals that envelope the soul
And heal the wounds

My arms enfold you, embrace you
And cherish you
I long to bring you to me

To reveal the inner petals and
The secrets within.
I am the lover of your soul
I call you to me
To receive my generous gifts
Not because you deserve
But because I love
And that is all I can do.

So hide not from me
Embrace me as I embrace you
Nestle into the petals
Smell the beauty as love unfolds
And takes you to the centre
Where the sweet smelling perfumes
Lure you onwards to loving perfection.

Drink in my nectar
Let its sugary taste sustain you
And bring joy to your senses
Let the spring unfold
And enjoy the love of God everywhere

The red rose is of spring
Where new life abounds
And new things are seen
And the grace of God falls upon you.

Ann writes: "After this I was able to accept God's love for me. I felt great joy within. All of me was delighted. I felt like I could have cried out from the mountaintop that God loves me. I have noticed that I do not feel separate from God like I did previously. God is within."

Ann was deeply moved by this poem. The sacred life speaks to her through her drawing of the red rose. The images of the pearl and the nectar also speak of the divine presence. These images speak of a deep intimacy with God that she had not previously known. It was not an experience fostered in her former religious affiliation. The poem invites her into the mystical tradition. She experiences God in the depths of her own soul. The imagery implies communing with God, through the intimate embrace and by drinking the nectar.

The poem confirms to Ann that, while she has left her former religious community, she continues to find meaning in a relationship with the God image grounded in her experience. For Ann the colour red symbolises energy and love, and in the Christian tradition it is associated with the Spirit of God. The rose symbol in western spirituality is often seen as the equivalent to the lotus of eastern spiritual traditions. These flowers symbolise the divine life, God for Ann. Given her family story presented earlier, this poem is a remarkable expression of the sacred centre in Ann's soul that she is now coming to know.

Many years ago a colleague and I were facilitating a conference over a weekend. On the Sunday morning we participated in the Eucharistic worship of the hosting church. My colleague was the preacher. He was a creative and spontaneous man and on this morning that energy came forward in a surprising way. On impulse in the course of his sermon, he left the pulpit, went to the altar, unveiled the vessels set for the communion, and held up the large host used by the priest. His question was something like: "How is it we can see Christ in this, and have trouble seeing Christ in each other?" It was a stunned and stunning moment that raised the ongoing question of our perceptions.

In this chapter we have reviewed stories that remind us of the infinite ways in which the deep voice of wisdom may choose to speak to us from the depths of the unconscious. Name it as we will – Spirit, the divine life, the deep voice of wisdom, God, Christ, or the holy ones of any tradition or of our personal history – the encounters bring us opportunities for a greater self-understanding, for developing a stronger sense of personal authority, a greater freedom to act from our conscious intentions, and the relief of making peace with ourselves.

It is not unusual for us, especially in faith circles, to view with hesitation any new image or idea associated with Divinity that invites us beyond our present understanding and our received tradition. If we can hold these images quietly and reflect on their influence we may find they provide us with whole new ways of seeing. These new images also offer us the opportunity to move beyond a narrow sense of self into a larger, more complex and varied self-understanding. This likewise makes it possible for us to engage the diversity and complexity of others with greater interest and ease. The challenge here is to have the courage to accept that the Spirit will choose whatever image is best for our healing, including images well outside the usual expectations and boundaries of our faith traditions.

As we have seen in the dialogues in these chapters, the necessary insights we need for our continued growth into our wholeness may come in a wide variety of ways and at times unsettle us. Along with the specific images of the faith traditions, the sacred life may speak to us through our anxiety, loneliness, our ideal self, or speak to us through the images of the elephant, lion, black beetle, impala or bear, or even seek our attention through the aches and pains of parts of our bodies.

The ancient practice of discernment is helpful in assessing the value of any new images and voices that speak. Simple questions serve us in determining how to regard the insights that emerge.

Does the unexpected image invite us to a deeper self-understanding?

Does this image strengthen our sense of wellness, and personal authority?

Do the images convey the essence of the one it claims to represent?

Does this new image enable us to relate to others with a greater compassion?

These and other questions will help us assess the value and benefit of the images that emerge in active imagination; images that take us beyond the present boundaries of our understanding, and challenge us to settle into a deeper, more rich and vibrant sense of the sacred life, of our own self, of our views of others, and the larger world.

Afterword

We're all so many people, aren't we, nowadays?
Georgina Harding

Yet we actually read literature, we go to art,
we watch movies to discover we are not just one person
but a million possibilities.
Richard Flanagan

Do I contradict myself? Very well then I contradict myself,
I am large, I contain multitudes.
Walt Whitman

Just over twenty years ago I woke in the middle of the night and found a poem of sorts emerging in my half-awake state. I got up early that morning and wrote out what had emerged as best I could recall. After that I worked with it a bit and the result is the following poetic reflection on my experience of active imagination up to that point in my life. I have decided to use it here as the last word about active imagination in my experience. I have decided not to update it, but let it stand as created that

morning. It offers insight into the impact over time of this spirited
and transforming practice.

WHO ARE THESE?

1.

Who are these
who arrive in my dreams, or
　　who emerge from the shades of the Abyss,
who haunt my waking hours
　　with their strange ways and
　　their unexpected points of view?

Who are these …
　　so intimate,
　　so close my skin seems distant
　　from my body when I compare,
who know me deeply, yet do not flinch
　　in my presence as sometimes do I,
who are these who ask no shame,
and only such guilt that moves me
　　along a way I cannot see,
　　in which they believe?

Who are these
who believe so deeply in me, and
who, without sentiment or put down,
lift me up with unending support
　　for whoever it is I am meant to be?

Who are these
who come, and frighten and console me,
who demand and who give,
who leave me wondering,
with my feet more firmly placed
    on the pathway of my own life?

Who are these
who at differing moments offer me no comfort,
and yet who are such deep comfort
    in the face of life's confusions?

Who are these
who variously strike fear into my heart and
    cause the sweet heart ache of knowing love,
who accept me and support me,
who cry my tears when I am weary or aggrieved,
who scream my agonies and rages,
my "Whys?" at a silent and
    sometimes indifferent cosmos
     yet who seem a cosmos within?

                        Who are these?

Who are these
who whisper sweet somethings in my ear,
who insist on their truth and
    counsel my obedience?

Who are these
who sometimes are angry and aggressive
    in the face of my neglect,
yet whose hostility turns quickly when I turn to notice?

Who are these
who present me with oracles and imperatives –
    "you must understand this..."
    "Listen ..."
    "Do this ..."
    "be patient ..."
    "stay with the vision ...?"

Who are these
who welcome me warmly
on my coming to their place within,
a place that is no place,
a kind of home beyond all homes –
    refuge ... sanctuary ... haven

    on the beach
    in a darkened room or
        a prison cell,
    at a small camp fire,
    on a rock by the stream?

Who are these ...
    Dog,
    the wild-eyed shaman with whom I dance,
    Power storming in a cell,
    Anger smashing chairs,

the witch at her cauldron,
the beautiful maiden,
the old nun and silent monk,
the wise old man,
the munchkin gardener with one tomato to tend,
contempt,
the menacing men,
the youth with the knife,
the chieftain,
the man emerging from the smoke,
the voice,
she who takes the feminine of my name,
my own back spewing the anger over things held in too many years,
a mob of boys whose ages tell the story of woundings past,
a Christ
      whose unchristly ways
      offer me strange consolation and
      leave me in silent wonderment,

these and many others,
the "other" within,
a family unknown before their appearings,
surprising familiars,
                 Who are these?

Who are these,
and because they are these,
                 Who am I?

2.

These are they,
the unexpected,
who surprise me with their comings and
     who leave well-being, contentment,
     insight and peace in their goings.

These are they,
who expand my sense of self,
who enrich me with variety, complexity,
     opposition, even conflicting points of view,
who insist that differing perspectives,
     ambivalent responses and
     passionate struggles are preferred
     to the boredom of the singular.

These are they
who come to teach, challenge, guide, enlighten,
     who cultivate dialogue and mutuality between us,
who strive for negotiation, reconciliation,
     a deep harmony in me,
     a working family in which we all get a hearing.

These are they
who speak truth,
truths tailored for my soul –
     "All is one is essence"
     "get back to the earth"
     "live from your soul"
     "you have much deep truth in you" –

truths that are not unique,
but that become mine.

These are they
who feel outside my sense of control
who come as gifts themselves yet
who counsel hard work and gritty effort.

These are they
my denied, my lost, my forgotten, my never known,
    my family who with me compose
    a self of astonishing satisfaction.

These are they
who are committed to truth in the inward places,
who speak the honest word to liberate and to heal.

These are they,
fringe dwellers,
liminal, transgressive,
breaking boundaries, crossing borders,
by outer standards unconventional, strange and lawless,
these are they who affirm the truth from within,
who demand fidelity to the ways of the soul.

These are they, and
because they are these,

I am who I am.

My hope in creating this study is that many will discover here a
way to move beyond the "boredom of the singular" and engage

positively the wondrous complexity of the human experience. Active imagination, as Jung says, is a way to "make enemies friends," that is, to come to a peaceful, affirming and loving relationship with all the complex characters that make up our lives over time. It is also a mediative way to listen to our deepest dreams and hopes, and to engage the adventure of a more whole life. To engage ourselves more fully, and with increasing compassion, will increase our capacity to engage others and indeed the entire creation with the disciplined intention to celebrate and work for the good health of all others and of the environment. The benefits of engaging ourselves with respect are far reaching in contributing to the increased health of humanity and the renewed well-being of our planet home. This sacred, life-giving journey often begins by turning in with care and asking, "Who said that?"

Acknowledgements

In addition to the people who have contributed their work to this study, I also acknowledge and thank those many others who have engaged the adventure of active imagination during their work with me and have shared the benefits and riches of their experiences. The learning has been mutual, and I am grateful.

I acknowledge with gratitude Weyler Greene, the Jungian Analyst who first introduced me to this practice. Little did we know what passion would ignite in me when I entered this realm of the imagination. I am grateful to Morton Kelsey who added a depth of understanding of the sacred nature of this experience. I am deeply grateful to Dr. Peter Bedford who encouraged me to pursue a PhD around this practice, and to Dr. Sally Kester who kept niggling me to write up what I shared in our many conversations. My gratitude extends as well to my supervisors at Edith Cowan University, Dr Cynthia Dixon and Dr. Pat Baines, who supported me through that adventure, that resulted in my PhD being awarded in 2000. Each of these, in her or his way, has contributed support and encouragement to my ongoing exploration of active imagination that now results in this study. I am also grateful to Ann Wilson at Independent Ink, and her colleagues Michelle Van Dyk and Julian Mole for their focused attention to detail and their collaboration, counsel and guidance in bringing my vision for this work to production. In the time of Covid they have persevered to produce the book and have also given me a great learning experience. It's been a pleasure.

References

Hannah, Barbara. (1981). *Encounters with the Soul: Active Imagination*. Santa Monica: Sigo Press.

Hillman, James. (1995). A Psyche the Size of the Earth: A Psychological Foreward. in *Ecopsychology: Restoring the Earth Healing the Mind*, Theodore Roszak, Ed. San Francisco: Sierra Club Books.

Johnson, Robert (1986). *Inner Work: Using Dreams and Active Imagination for Personal Growth*. San Francisco: HarperSanFrancisco.

Kelsey, Morton, T. (1995). *The Other Side of Silence: Meditation for the Twenty-First Century*. New York: Paulist Press.

O'Donohue, John. (1997/2004). *Anam Cara: A Book of Celtic Wisdom*. New York: Harper Perennial.

Sanford, John. (1994). *Mystical Christianity: A Psychological Commentary on the Gospel of John*. New York: Crossroad.

Watkins, Mary. (1986). *Invisible guests: The Devlopment of Imaginal Dialogues*. Hillsdale: The Analytic Press.

Further Reading

From Jung's Collected Works:
R. F. C. Hull, Trans. Princeton: Princeton University Press.
Listed in order by date, volume and paragraphs.
(1916a/1966). The relations between the ego and the unconscious.
　Vol. 7, para. 202-406.
(1916b/1969). The Transcendent Function. Vol. 8, para. 131-193.
(1934/1969). A Study in the Process of Individuation. Vol. 9,
　part 1, para. 525-626.
(1936/1969). The Concept of the Collective Unconscious. Vol. 9,
　Part 1, para. 87-110.
(1948/1969). The Phenomenology of the Spirit in Fairytales.
　Vol. 9, Part 1 para. 384-455.
(1951/1969). The psychological aspects of the kore. Vol. 9, Part 1,
　para. 306-383.
(1954a/1966). General problems of psychotherapy. Vol. 16, para.
　1-254.
(1954b/1970). Mysterium Coniunctionis. Vol. 14, para 706.

From Jung's Letters
Letters 1. 1906-1950. Ed: Gerhard Adler, Trans. R. F. C. Hull.
London: Routledge & Regan Paul. pp. 82-83.

From other writers
Dallett, Janet. (1982.) Active imagination in practice. In M. Stein,
　(Ed.),
Jungian Analysis. La Salle: Open Court. pp. 173-191.
Dieckmann, H. (1979/1991). *Methods in analytical psychology*.
　Wilmette, Ill: Chiron Publications.

Franz, M-L. von. (1974/1980). *Shadow and evil in fairytales.* Irving, Texas: Spring Publications, Inc.

Hannah, Barbara. (1953). Some remarks on active imagination. In *Spring,* 1953.pp. 38-58.

Humbert, E. (1971). Active Imagination: Theory and Practice. In *Spring,*

1971, pp. 101-114.

Shea, John. (1993). *Starlight: Beholding the Christmas Miracle All Year Long.*

New York: Crossroad.

Storr, Anthony. (1988). *Solitude: A Return to the Self.* New York: Ballantine Books.

www.ingramcontent.com/pod-product-compliance
Lightning Source LLC
Chambersburg PA
CBHW072125020426
42334CB00018B/1709